# Detroit Studies in
# Music Bibliography

General Editor
**Bruno Nettl**
University of Illinois at Urbana-Champaign

DETROIT STUDIES IN MUSIC BIBLIOGRAPHY NUMBER THIRTY-SEVEN

# ITALIAN BAROQUE SOLO SONATAS FOR THE RECORDER AND THE FLUTE

by

Richard A. McGowan

Information Coordinators

Book design by Vincent Kibildis.
Cover and title page illustration
adapted from two illustrations in
Hotteterre-le-Romain's
*Principes de la flute traversiere . . .*
*de la flute a bec . . .*
*et du haut-bois*, 1707.

# CONTENTS

# ACKNOWLEDGMENTS

I wish to express my thanks to all of the persons who helped me in the preparation of this work, including the directors and staff members of the many libraries and museums who provided microfilms, photographs, and other materials.  For their special assistance, I am particularly indebted to Laura Newsom, François Lesure, Pierluigi Petrobelli, William C. Smith, and Robert A. Warner; and, above all, I am indebted to the Horace Rackham School of Graduate Studies at the University of Michigan for the research grant that enabled me to undertake this work.

# INTRODUCTION

The interest of flutists in preclassical music has increased considerably during recent years. The growth may be credited to editors and publishers who have made early works much more accessible and to those persons who have provided informative reference works on the history of music publishing and early woodwind literature. Some of the most notable contributions in the latter category are Hugo Alker's *Blockflöten-Bibliographie,* Martin Loonan's "A Listing of Late Baroque Solo Sonatas for the Alto Recorder," Frans Vester's *Flute Repertoire Catalogue,* and L. H. von Winterfeld's *Handbuch der Blockflöten-Literatur.*[1]

The present bibliography is more specialized than most reference works of this kind. It is concerned only with baroque solo sonatas by Italian composers who lived in Italy or, as immigrants, in other European countries. Moreover, it is restricted to works that, according to their titles, are specifically or primarily intended for the recorder or the flute.

The bibliography is in two parts. The first part lists and describes eighteenth century editions and manuscripts. Included are the locations of sources and,

---

[1] Hugh Alker, *Blockflöten-Bibliographie* (Wilhelmshaven: Heinrichshofen, 1966) with a supplement and index (1969); Martin A. Loonan, "A Listing of Late Baroque Solo Sonatas for Alto Recorder," *The American Recorder* XII/no. 3 (August 1971), 86-90; Frans Vester, *Flute Repertoire Catalogue* (London: Musica Rara, 1967); and Linde Hoffer von Winterfeld, *Handbuch der Blockflöten-Literatur* (Berlin: Bote & Bock, 1959).

when known, library catalog numbers. The second section contains modern editions. Further details are given in the remarks at the beginnings of the two sections.

Upon examining the historical editions, one observes that, characteristically, most sonatas were published in sets of six or twelve. During the first quarter of the century, the bulk of these publications were for the recorder, the more popular instrument at that time. By the late 1720's, however, the *traversa* was proving itself a superior instrument, attributable to its greater flexibility of expression and its essentially sharp-key tonality, which is more compatible with string instruments. Thus the repertory of the *traversa* grew rapidly. In some cases sonatas originally written for the recorder, such as those of Benedetto Marcello, were adapted for the flute (see pp. 32-33).

Most of the publishing occurred in Holland, England, and later, France. Here editions were attractively engraved in score, using modern clefs and providing quite fully figured *basso continuo* parts. Comparatively little music was published in Italy, where printers still adhered to the centuries old process of single-impression, movable type.

Northern publishers were enterprising not only in their printing techniques, but also in their advertising, issuing numerous catalogs, many of which contained sections of music for the flute. During the second quarter of the century some publishers also issued special lists of flute music.[2] One must understand, however, that while the lists for certain instruments were oftentimes neatly classified, such listings would have been nearly impossible in the cases of the recorder and the flute; their repertories were simply too conglomerate. Early catalogs typically intermixed French airs, trios, and other diverse pieces in a single section. Even after 1725 publishers not infrequently grouped sonatas and other works under headings including the flute, the oboe, and the violin.

As a result the early repertory of flute music is confused, a situation that is complicated by the sometimes deliberate attempt of a publisher to obscure the original opus number, medium, or composer of a work. Changes in titles and opus numbers are fairly common as are alternate and revised title pages—all of which tend to encourage multiple catalog listings. In addition, a number of works were pirated by various publishers. One noteworthy example of this practice concerns a collection of twelve sonatas entitled *Solos for the German Flute . . . fitted . . . by Pietro Chaboud,* the contents of which were later misrepresented to be by Francesco Geminiani and Pietro Castrucci. The original edition was printed by John Walsh of London ca. 1725 and subsequently reprinted by him ca. 1730. About this same time the Amsterdam publisher, Michel-Charles Le Cène, an aggressive competitor of Walsh, apparently recognized

---

[2] See William C. Smith and Charles Humphries, *A Bibliography of the Musical Works Published by the Firm of John Walsh during the Years 1721-1726* (London: The Bibliographical Society, 1968), p. xii.

in this collection two sonatas from the first opuses of Geminiani and Castrucci (which both Walsh and Le Cène had published earlier in several editions). Either believing that the ten remaining sonatas in the collection, whose authorship is presently unknown, were also by Geminiani and Castrucci, or wishing to represent them as such, Le Cène published the collection himself, ca. 1731, entitling it *XII Sonate a flauto traversie . . . dei Gli Sign. Francesco Geminiani é Castrucci.* Walsh, who recognized the greater commercial appeal of Le Cène's title, responded by engraving a new title page for his edition and reissued the collection ca. 1743 as *XII Solos for a German Flute . . . by Sigr. Geminiani and Castrucci.* Thus numerous misattributions of these sonatas to Geminiani and Castrucci have resulted [3] and one can only wonder how many other works may be similarly misrepresented.

Needless to say, with problems like this, one recognizes that much additional research in woodwind literature is needed and that a bibliography such as this one represents only a beginning. For one thing, several editions are still lost (see Appendix, pp. 61-62). In addition, the reader is advised that the manuscript sources included in this study have been located primarily through printed library catalogs, not by direct investigation. Thus works in manuscript are no doubt considerably underrepresented.

---

[3] See, for example, Francesco Geminiani, "Sonata E-moll für Oboe oder Querflöte oder Violine und Basso continuo," ed. Hugo Ruf, in the series, *Hortus Musicus,* no. 178 (Kassel: Bärenreiter, 1961). For additional information, see Richard A. McGowan, "Italian Baroque Solo Sonatas for the Recorder and the Flute," (unpublished Ph.D. dissertation, The University of Michigan, 1974), pp. 178-83.

# LIBRARY SIGLA

| | |
|---|---|
| **A** Wn | Vienna, Österreichische Nationalbibliothek |
| **B** Bc | Brussels, Bibliothèque du Conservatoire Royal de Musique |
| **D-brd** B-MG | Marburg, Staatsbibliothek der Stiftung Preussischer Kulturbesitz, Depot Marburg |
| **D-brd** JE | Jever, Bibliothek des Marien-Gymnasiums |
| **D-brd** KA | Karlsruhe, Badische Landesbibliothek |
| **D-brd** Mbs | Munich, Bayerische Staatsbibliothek |
| **D-brd** WD | Wiesentheid, Graf von Schönborn'sche Musikbibliothek |
| **D-ddr** Bds | Berlin, Deutsche Staatsbibliothek |
| **D-ddr** LEm | Leipzig, Musikbibliothek der Stadt Leipzig |
| **D-ddr** SW1 | Schwerin, Mecklenburgische Landesbibliothek |
| **DK** Kk | København, Det kongelige Bibliotek |
| **F** Pc | Paris, Bibliothèque Nationale, fonds du Conservatoire |
| **F** Pn | Paris, Bibliothèque Nationale |
| **GB** Ckc | Cambridge, Rowe Music Library, King's College |
| **GB** Cu | Cambridge, University Library |
| **GB** CDp | Cardiff, Public Libraries, Central Library |

| | |
|---|---|
| **GB** DRc | Durham, Cathedral Library |
| **GB** En | Edinburg, National Library of Scotland |
| **GB** Er | Edinburgh, Reid Music Library of the University of Edinburgh |
| **GB** Lbm | London, British Museum (i.e., the British Library) |
| **GB** Lcm | London, Royal College of Music |
| **GB** Lk | London, King's Music Library (British Library) |
| **GB** LEc | Leeds, Public Libraries, Music Department, Central Library |
| **GB** LVu | Liverpool, University Music Department |
| **GB** Mp | Manchester, Central Public Library |
| **GB** Ob | Oxford, Bodleian Library |
| **GB** Oc | Oxford, Coke Collection |
| **GB** T | Tenbury, St. Michael's College Library |
| **I** Bc | Bologna, Civico Museo Bibliografico Musicale (Liceo Musicale) |
| **I** BGi | Bergamo, Istituto musicale "Donizetti" |
| **I** Gl | Genova, Biblioteca del Liceo Musicale "Paganini" |
| **I** PAc | Parma, Sezione Musicale della Biblioteca Palatina |
| **I** Vqs | Venice, Biblioteca dell'Accademia Querini-Stampalia |
| **NL** DHgm | Den Haag, Gemeente Museum |
| **NL** Lu | Leiden, Universiteits-Bibliotheek |
| **NZ** Wt | Wellington, The Alexander Turnbull Library |
| **S** Skma | Stockholm, Kungliga Musikaliska Academiens Bibliotek |
| **S** SK | Skara, Stifts- och Landsbiblioteket |
| **S** Uu | Uppsala, Universitetsbiblioteket |
| **US** AA | Ann Arbor, Music Library, University of Michigan |
| **US** NH | New Haven, School of Music Library, Yale University |
| **US** NYp | New York, New York Public Library at Lincoln Center |
| **US** R | Rochester, Sibley Music Library, Eastman School of Music |
| **US** Wc | Washington, Library of Congress, Music Division |

# EIGHTEENTH CENTURY EDITIONS AND MANUSCRIPTS

The following sources are arranged alphabetically by composer and, whenever possibly, by opus number. Published editions of works are listed first, chronologically, followed by manuscripts. The descriptive procedures for editions and manuscripts differ somewhat. In the case of the editions, the title pages have been lined out. A single slash (/) signifies the termination of each line of text; a double slash (//) indicates the presence of a long, separative line or ornament. Second, although no attempt is made to indicate the relative sizes of letters, the original usage of capital and lower case letters is preserved. Moreover, words in italics are denoted by sans serif italics (e.g., *CON BASSO PER VIOLONE O CEMBALO*); words in script, by serif italics (e.g., *Printed for & sold by I: Walsh*). The publisher's imprint, plate number, date, and other information given on the title page are included. Editorial omissions are indicated by ellipses. The number of sonatas in the edition, the publication or privilege date, and other various details are added in brackets when they are otherwise not given. Lacking further description, an edition may be assumed to be engraved in an upright score format. The copy which has been examined is identified below the title-page entry, using the respective library *siglum* adopted by the International Musicological Society and the International Association of Music Libraries in the series, *Répertoire internationale des sources musicales* (*R.i.s.m.*). Immediately following is a description, indicating the presence of a title page, a dedication, an *avertissement,* a publisher's catalog, and the number of pages of music. The locations of other known copies of the publication are listed separately below. Library call numbers are included in parentheses. Annotations follow, giving information about the composer, the work, and the edition.

The manuscripts are identified by title, library, and catalog number. Also indicated are the numbers of pages, including music and title pages. Supplementary information is added in brackets, but lining out and other descriptive techniques are not used. Annotations contain further information, in some cases biographical facts. Except when indicated otherwise, the format of a manuscript is horizontal.

Two libraries possess especially noteworthy manuscripts, the Biblioteca Palatina in Parma (**I PAc**), and the Biblioteca dell'Accademia Querini-Stampalia in Venice (**I Vqs**). Among the holdings of the Biblioteca Palatina is a volume of miscellaneous manuscripts entitled *Sinfonie de varij autori,*[1] which contains twenty-six instrumental chamber compositions, mostly works for recorder. Included are manuscripts of twenty-two solo recorder sonatas, four of them anonymous, and an anonymous set of twenty-six variations on *La Follia,* all apparently in the hands of two copyists, hereafter identified as A and B. Not all of the sonatas are original works for the recorder, however. Three of them are transcriptions of violin sonatas, two by Tomaso Albinoni and one attributed to Arcangelo Corelli.[2] This fact suggests that other sonatas in the collection were originally intended for the violin, a view that certain idiomatic characteristics tend to support.

The Biblioteca dell'Accademia Querini-Stampalia also contains a volume of recorder music. This collection,[3] which displays the work of three copyists, hereafter identified as C, D, and E, consists of seven solo sonatas, four of which are anonymous.

---

[1] Catalogue no. CF-V-23, listed as "Raccolta di Sonate di Diversi" in Guido Gasperini and Nestore Pellicelli (comps.), *Catalogo delle città di Parma e Reggio,* Vol. I of *Catalogo generale . . . ,* published by the Associazione dei Musicologi Italiani (Parma: Freschig, 1911), p. 257.

[2] Compositions nos. 1 and 11 in the collection are adaptations of Sonatas VI and IX from Albinoni's *Trattenimenti per camera a due,* Op. VI (Amsterdam: Roger, [ca. 1708-1712]). See François Lesure, *Bibliographie des éditions musicales publiées par Estienne Roger et Michel-Charles Le Cène (Amsterdam, 1696-1743),* Vol. XII of *Publications de la Société Française de Musicologie,* Series II (Paris: Société Française de Musicologie, 1969), p. 58. Sonata no. 14 is an adaptation of Sonata IV published in *Sonate a Violino Solo col B. C. composte da Arcangelo Corelli e altri autory* (Amsterdam: Roger, 1697). See Marc Pincherle, *Corelli, His Life, His Work,* translated from the French by Hubert E. M. Russell (New York: W. W. Norton & Co., Inc., 1956), p. 219 and Lesure, *Bibliographie,* p. 64.

[3] Catalogue no. Cl. VIII, Cod. 27, listed as "Album musicale di pezzi varii p. Flauto solo e B. C." in Giovanni Concina (comp.), *Catalogo della Biblioteca Querini-Stampalia di Venezia,* Vol. VI of *Catalogo generale . . .* (Parma: Freschig, 1914), p. 5.

## ANONYMOUS SONATAS

*Sonata [in re min.] à flauto solo*
A Wn. Estense coll., No. 66. Ms. parts. 4 fols.

*Sinfonia [in fa magg.] à flauto solo, e basso*
I PAc. *Sinfonie* Mss. (CF-V-23), fols. 43r.-45r.
In the hand of copyist A; bass partially figured; few interpretive markings.

*Sinfonia [in do magg.] à flauto solo*
I PAc. *Sinfonie* Mss. (CF-V-23), fols. 45v.-46v.
In the hand of copyist A; bass unfigured. The perpetual motion of the first movement and the passage work of the allegro movements suggest that the work may have been written originally for violin.

*Sinfonia [in fa magg.] à flauto solo, e basso*
I PAc. *Sinfonie* Mss. (CF-V-23), fols. 51r.-54r.
In the hand of copyist A; bass almost wholly unfigured; few interpretive markings. The second and third minuets are scored in a simple *concertante* fashion, predominantly in parallel thirds.

*Sinfonia [in fa magg.] à flauto solo e basso*
I PAc. *Sinfonie* Mss. (CF-V-23), fols. 55r.-56v.
In the hand of copyist A; bass unfigured; solo part floridly elaborated.

*Sonate [in re min.] à flauto solo*
I Vqs. Ms. Cl. VIII, Cod. 27 [No. 3]. 4 pp.
In the hand of copyist D; bass unfigured; few interpretive markings.

*Sonata [in fa magg.] à flauto solo*
I Vqs. Ms. Cl. VIII, Cod. 27, [No. 4]. 6 pp.
In the hand of copyist E; quite precisely notated, but with few interpretive markings.

*Sinfonia 2 [in do magg.]*
I Vqs. Ms. Cl. VIII, Cod. 27, [No. 5]. 4 pp.
In the hand of copyist E; bass unfigured; few interpretive markings.

*Sinfonia 3 [in fa magg.]*
I Vqs. Ms. Cl. VIII, Cod. 27, [No. 6]. 5 pp.
In the hand of copyist E; bass unfigured; slurring (bowing?) quite fully marked.

*Sinfonia 4 [in sol magg.]*
I Vqs. Ms. Cl. VIII, Cod. 27, [No. 7]. 1 p. incomplete.
In the hand of copyist E; bass unfigured.

BARSANTI, FRANCESCO
Op. I

[VI] SONATE / *A FLAUTO, o VIOLINO SOLO* / *CON' BASSO, PER*
*VIOLONE, o CEMBALO.* / DEDICATE / ALL' ECCELLENZA DI MY
LORD / RICCARDO CONTE DI BURLINGTON, E CORK, / BARONE
CLIFFORD *DI* LANDESTROUGH, E / GRAN' TESORIERE *DEL* REGNO
D'IRLANDA *&c* / *DA* / *FRANCESCO BARSANTI* [London, 1924]
*Source:* GB Lbm (g. 261. a.) Title page, dedication, and 35 pages of music
*Another copy:* B Bc (T 12,116)

The dedication reads:

My LORD

Spero, che Vr̃a Eccza. mi perdonerà l'ardire ch'io mi prendo di
consacrare al Suo Merito qt̃e mie Sonate; l'Amore, e l'Intelligenza
Singolare, che V. E. hà di tutte le belle arti, e la Benignità, e
Grandezza d'animo ch'Ella dimostra in protéggerne i Professori,
ed i molti, e grandi beneficci, ch'io hò da Léi ricevuti m'an fatto
superare la reflessione della picciolezza mia, e del poco pregio del
dono, massime essendo per me impossibile il dimostrare altrimenti
la viva mia riconoscenza, e devozione verso l'E. Vr̃a, cui prego Iddio,
che per bene universale conservi lungo tempo felice.—
Londra li 8 Aprẽ 1724.
Di Vr̃a Eccz.
Umilmo. Devotmo. ed Obligmo. Servitore
Francesco Barsanti.

The following advertisement appeared in a newspaper of 1724:

This day is published Sonatas for a Flute, or Violin and Bass . . .
Composed by Sig. Barsanti, printed for the author and sold by
Mr. Bressan, musical instrument maker, at the Green door, in
Somerset House Yard, in the Strand, price 5s.[4]

Barsanti (ca. 1690-ca. 1760), born in Lucca, became quite successful as a
flutist-composer, especially after 1714 when he emigrated to London. There
he acquired a position as flutist, and subsequently oboist, at the King's Theatre.
Later he moved to Scotland where he worked for an undetermined number
of years. Returning to London ca. 1750, he resumed playing in the opera
and also played in the orchestra at Vauxhall Gardens, but this time as a violist.
In addition to performing and composing, Barsanti compiled two collections of
concertos transcribed from sonatas by Francesco Geminiani and G. B. Sammartini,
and also published a set of trios by the latter composer.

---

[4] Quoted in Frank Kidson, *British Music Publishers, Printers and Engravers* (London:
W. E. Hill & Sons, 1900), p. 224.

**Second Edition**

SONATAS / *or* / SOLOS / *for a* / FLUTE / *with a* / THOROUGH BASS / *for the* / HARPSICORD / *or* / BASS VIOLIN / *Compos'd by* / FRANCESCO BARSANTI / / ... / / *London. Printed for & sold by I: Walsh servant to his Majesty at* / *ỹ Harp and Hoboy in Catherine street in ỹ Strand. and Joseph Hare* / *at ỹ Viol and Flute in Cornhill near the Royal Exchange.* [1727]

*Source:* **GB** Lbm (g. 70. c. (1.)) Title page, with the price 0.3.0 noted after the imprint, and 35 pages of music

*Another copy:* **GB** DRc

**BARSANTI, FRANCESCO**
**Op. II**

VI / SONATE / *PER LA TRAVERSIERA, O GERMAN FLUTE,* / *CON BASSO PER VIOLONE O CEMBALO* / *Dedicate* / ALL' ECCELLENZA DI MY LORD / MARCHESE DI BLANDFORD / *da* / *Francesco Barsanti* / OPERA SECONDA / / LONDON / *Printed for & Sold by* Ben Cooke *at the Golden Harp in New Street Covt Gard:* / ... [1728]

*Source:* **GB** Lbm (g. 261. b.) Title page, dedication, and 31 pages of music

*Another copy:* **GB** LEc

The dedication reads:

My Lord

L'ardire di mettere sotto gl'auspicii di Vostra Eccellenza queste mie Sonate nasce non solo dalla gran Bontà, che nella Vostra Persona riluce, ma dal desio altresi di renderle grate al publico fregiandole col nome d'un soggetto, i di cui nobili talenti lo fanno a tutti riguardevole. Le stimerei felici, se fossero accolte da V. Eza. colla stessa benignità, che più volte mostrommi, e che mi á con ogn' ossequio perpetuamente costituito
Di Vrã Eccza

Londra Li 12 Giugno 1728

Umilissmo. ed Obedietissmo. Servitore
Francesco Barsanti

Parker Sculpet.

Compared to Parker's finely engraved dedication, the music is crudely done. Furthermore, the above copy is marred with casual handwritten trill signs, measure numbers, and other markings.

**BARSANTI, FRANCESCO**
**Op. II, Second Edition**

> SOLOS / *for a* / GERMAN FLUTE / *a* HOBOY *or* VIOLIN /
> *with a* / *Thorough Bass for the* / HARPSICHORD / *or* / BASS
> VIOLIN / *Compos'd by* / Francesco Barsanti / Opera Terza / /
> *N.B. The rest of the Works of this Author may be had where*
> *these are sold* / *Also great variety of new Musick for the German*
> *Flute* / / *London. Printed for and sold by I: Walsh servant to*
> *his Majesty at the Harp* / *and Hoboy in Catherine street in*
> *the Strand.* / *N$\underline{o}$ 355* [Second printing? ca. 1732]
>
> *Source:* **GB** Lbm (g. 270. 1. (1.) )   Title page and 31 pages of music
>
> *Other copies:* **B** Bc (T 12,117); **US** Wc (M 242 .B26 Op. 3)

The imprint of the copy in the Library of Congress includes:

> *and Joseph Hare at the Viol* / *and Hoboy in Cornhill near the*
> *Royal Exchange*

and excludes the plate number, indicating a first printing of 1728.

Barsanti's *traversa* sonatas were also advertised by John Johnson ca. 1754
and later by Robert Bremner who acquired many of Johnson's plates from his
widow in 1777. Whether Johnson sold his own edition or perhaps that of Walsh
is not certain.[5]

**Another Edition**

> FOUR SONATAS / FOR THE / GERMAN FLUTE. / With an
> / *Accompaniment for the* / *Violoncello or Harpsichord.* /
> Composed by / *Sig$\underline{r}$ Barsanti.* / / London: [ca. 1780]
>
> *Source:* **US** Wc (Miller Collection, ML 30.4, No. 2128). Obl. 6⅜x 9¼
> inches. Title page and 24 pages of music numbered as pages 3-26.
> Contains Sonatas I-IV in the original order. Bound together with
> Samuel Arnold's *New Instructions for the German-Flute* (1787).
>
> *Another copy:* **NZ** Wt?

---

[5] See John Johnson, "A Catalogue of Vocal and Instrumental Musick" (London
[ca. 1754]; Brit. Mus., Hirsch IV. 1111. (9.) ), [p. 1] and Robert Bremner, "A Catalogue
of Vocal and Instrumental Music" (London: March 1782; Brit. Mus., Hirsch IV. 1112.
(2.) ), p. 2. There is considerable duplicity among the works advertised by Johnson and
Walsh. In the case of these solos, moreover, Johnson, too, lists the work as Op. 3.

**Manuscript**

*Sonate a flauto, o violino solo con basso per violone o cembalo del sig.ʳ Francesco Barsanti*
I PAc. Ms. 35078-CA-II-11. Obl. fol.

Containing 47 pages of music and in the hand of copyist A. An outside title page (*recto*) is lettered *Sinfonie Di Francesco Barsanti,* of which the *verso* is marked "Di Paolo Ant.ᵒ Parensi."

**BELLINZANI, PAOLO BENEDETTO**
**Op. III**

[XII] SONATE / A FLAUTO SOLO / CON CEMBALO, O VIOLONCELLO
/ *DEDICATE AGL' ILLUSTRISSIMI SIGNORI* / JACOPO TESSARINI, /
E / FRANCESCO BERTOLI / DA PAOLO BENEDETTO BELLINZANI /
Maestro di Cappella della Cattedrale di Udine. / OPERA TERZA. / /
IN VENEZIA, M.DCCXX. / Appresso Antonio Bortoli a San Lorenzo.
/ *CON LICENZA DE' SUPERIORI.* [obl. fol. printed from movable type]

*Source:* I Bc (DD. 261) Title page, dedication, advice to the performers, 56 (originally 58) pages of music, and a catalog. Lacking are two pages, fol. 4, *recto* and *verso,* presumably containing the last two movements of the third sonata.

Bellinzani, a composer of sacred vocal and instrumental works, was apparently born at Mantua or Ferrara ca. 1690. Working at many posts, he lived successively at Udine, Ferrara, Pesaro, Urbino, Fano, Orvieto, and finally Recanati, where he died in 1757.[6]

---

[6] For further details about Bellinzani's life and works, see Carlo Schmidl, *Dizionario universale dei musicisti,* I (Milan: Casa Editrice Sonzogno, 1928), 248; Robert Eitner, *Biographisch-Bibliographisches Quellen-Lexikon der Musiker und Musikgelehrten,* I (Leipzig: Breitkopf & Härtel, 1900), 426-27; H. Springer, M. Schneider, and W. Wolffheim, *Miscellanea Musicae Bio-bibliographica,* II (New York: Musurgia, 1947), 28; and Pierluigi Petrobelli, "Bellinzani, Paolo Benedetto," *Die Musik in Geschichte und Gegenwart,* ed. Friedrich Blume, XV (1973), 629-30.

The dedication to the above work reads:

ILLUSTRISSIMI SIGNORI.

Al egregio merito, e all' efficace Protezione delle Signorie Vostre
Illustrissime umilio questo debol parto del mio rozzo talento, sì
per attestato dei molti obblighi, che loro professo, come per averli
validi difensori contro i Zoili, & Aristarchi di questo secolo. Ed
in fatti a chi meglio potevano esser indirizzati i miei studj, che
alle Signorie Vostre Illustrissime, che quantunque applicate alle
Scienze più sublimi, non isdegnano dar mano tal volta à Concerti
di Musica, riuscendovi in quelli con piena ammirazione anco de'
più eccellenti in quest' Arte. Nobilissimo divertimento che fà
contrapunto alla bella armonia delle Virtù, che sì degnamente le
distinguono, e denota chiaramente quel loro Genio soave, da cui
mi prometto anch' io un generoso gradimento. Si compiacciano
adunque (siccome umilmente le supplico) di riguardar la presente
opera con quella parziale benignità con cui hanno sempre onorati
i miei deboli componimenti, e la mia inutile servitù. Questo sarà
il maggior compenso, che possa attendere la mia presente fatica;
poiche così certificato del lor sospirato Patrocinio, m'assicura
l'onore sempre bramato di farmi conoscere
Delle Signorie Vostre Illustrissime.

Umilissimo Servitore Obbligatissimo
Paolo Benedetto Bellinzani.

AL

The date of publication is sometimes given as 1728. This seems to be the
result of a printing error in the catalog of the Biblioteca del Liceo Musicale,[7]
for the edition itself clearly dates 1720 and identifies Bellinzani as the *Maestro
di cappella della cattedrale di Udine,* a position that the composer held until 1722.
Readers are advised that the opus does not, strictly speaking, contain twelve
sonatas, but rather, as in Corelli's fifth opus, eleven sonatas and a set of variations
based upon the popular *La Follia.* The latter composition is preceded by a
so-called *cembalo solo* (fol. 24, *verso*), which, unlike the rest of the edition,
is engraved. Advertised in later catalogs of Bortoli at eight *lire,* the edition is
a good example of early eighteenth-century Italian printing by movable type.

### Sigr. BIGI

*Sonata [in fa magg.] del Sigr. Bigi.*
I Vqs. Ms. Cl. VIII, Cod. 27, [No. 1]. 4 pp.

In the hand of copyist C; bass unfigured.

---

[7] Gaetano Gaspari (comp.), *Catalogo della Biblioteca del Liceo Musicale di Bologna,*
IV (Bologna: Regia Tipografia Fratelli Merlani, 1905), 84.

## BONI, GIOVANNI

[VI] SOLOS / *for a* / GERMAN FLUTE, / *a* HOBOY *or* VIOLIN, / *with a* / *Thorough Bass for the* / HARPSICORD / *or* / BASS VIOLIN. / *Compos'd by* / Sig: Giovanni Boni. / / [lengthy advertisement follows] ... / / London. *Printed for and sold by* I: Walsh *servant to his Majesty at the Harp &* / *Hoboy in Catherine street in the Strand, and* Ioseph Hare *at the Viol and Hoboy* / *in Cornhill near the Royal Exchange* [ca. 1728]

*Source:* **GB** Lbm (g. 1090. (2.)) Title page and 18 pages of music

The composer is presently known only by the above work.

## BOTTIGNONI, PAULLO

*Sinfonia [in fa magg.] à flauto solo, é basso*
I PAc. *Sinfonie* Mss. (CF-V-23), fols. 27r.-30r.

The composer is probably identical with Paolino Bottigone, a cellist who served at the Cathedral of Parma from 1705 to 1725 and performed at the palisade (*steccata*) in 1726.[8]

The above sonata, in the hand of copyist B, displays a bass that is almost wholly unfigured. The perpetual motion of the allegro movements suggests that the work may have been originally intended for violin.

## BRIVIO, GIUSEPPE FERDINANDO

Six / SOLOS / *Four for a* / GERMAN FLUTE *and a* BASS / *and two for a* / VIOLIN / *with a Thorough Bass for the* / HARPSICORD / *or* / BASS VIOLIN / *Compos'd by* / M: Handel / / Sig: Somis / Sig: Geminiani / / Sig: Brivio / / London. *Printed for and sold by* I: Walsh *servant to his Majesty at* y | Harp and Hoboy in Catharine *street in the Strand. and Ioseph* / *Hare at the Viol and Flute in Cornhill near the Royal Exchange.* [1730]

*Source:* **GB** Lbm (h. 2140. d. (3.)) Title page and 20 pages of music

*Other copies:* **GB** Cu (MR 380. a. 70. 4), En (BH. 233), LVu, Ob, Oc; **S** Skma; **US** Wc (M 178 .S6)

---

[8] Nestore Pellicelli, "Musicisti in Parma nel sec. XVIII.—La Cappella della Steccata—La Capella corale della Cattedrale," *Note d'archivio per la storia musicale,* XI/no. 1 (January-March 1934), 51.

Brivio, whose forenames are sometimes given as Carlo Francesco or Carlo Fernando, was a well known singer, teacher, and composer who lived for many years at Milan. Carlo Schmidl states that his dates are ca. 1700-ca. 1758.[9] Although he is known primarily for his operas, he may be identical to the man named Brevio (also Bervio), in the catalogs of J. LeClerc and those of Boivin and Ballard, who is credited with two books of trios for flutes, or violins, and *continuo*.[10]

The collection of six solo sonatas was first advertised in *The Daily Post* on July 22, 1730. The copies listed above represent this initial printing (**GB** Cu, En, Lbm, LVu, Oc; **S** Skma) and also a later reprinting of ca. 1731 (**US** Wc and **GB** Ob) that differs only by the erasure of Hare's imprint and the addition of the plate number 398.[11] Two sonatas in the collection are by Brivio, the fourth in D major, for the flute (pp. 12-13), and the sixth in G major, for the violin (pp. 18-20).

**CALIFANO, ARCANGELO**

> *Sonata [in re magg. à] flauta traverso solo e basso*
> **D-ddr** SW1. Ms. 1424. Upright format. parts. 6 pp.

Califano is an obscure figure who is known to have been a cellist in the Dresden *Kapelle* in the 1730s and to have composed a small group of instrumental works.[12]

The above work, hastily copied, exhibits an unfigured bass, although it is fairly well marked with ornaments and articulation.

---

[9] See Schmidl, I, 248; Jean Benjamine de LaBorde, *Essai sur la musique ancienne et moderne,* III (Paris: Eugene Onfroy, 1780), 306 and 172; Ernst Ludwig Gerber, *Neues historisch-biographisches Lexikon der Tonkünstler,* I (Leipzig: A. Kuehnel, 1812), 515-16; and Sergio Martinotti, "Brivio, Giuseppe Ferdinando," *Die Musik in Geschichte und Gegenwart,* XV (1973), 1093-94.

[10] See Schmidl, I, 248; Eitner, II, 195; Jean LeClerc, *Catalogue général de musique imprimée ou gravée en France ensemble de celle qui est gravée ou imprimée dans les pays étrangers . . . se vend à Paris chez le Sieur le Clerc* (Paris: 1737; Bib. Nat., Q 9036), p. 56; and *Catalogue de musique tant françoise qu'italiene imprimée ou gravée en France à Paris chez le Sieur Le Clerc* (Paris: 1742; Bib. Nat., 9037), p. 11. The first book of trios is preserved in the Bibliothèque Nationale, catalogued in Jules Écorchville, *Catalogue du fonds de musique ancienne de la Bibliothèque Nationale,* III (Paris: J. Terquem & Cie, 1912), 129. See and compare also Smith and Humphries, *Walsh, 1721-1766,* p. 62 and Martinotti, p. 1094.

[11] See William C. Smith and Charles Humphries, *Handel: A Descriptive Catalogue of the First Editions* (2nd ed.; New York: Barnes and Noble, 1970), pp. 241-42; Smith and Humphries, *Walsh, 1721-1766,* pp. 130 and 311; and *Répertoire internationale des sources musicales,* Series B, Vol. II: *Recueils imprimés du xviiie siècle* (Munich: G. Henle, 1964), pp. 361-62, which is in error about the date of the Library of Congress copy.

[12] Eitner, II, 282.

## CANUTI, GIOVANNI ANTONIO

*Sonata [in fa magg.] à flauto solo e basso*
I PAc. Ms. *Sinfonie* Mss. (CF-V-23), fols. 39r.-42r.

Canuti (ca. 1680-1739), known mainly for his oratorios, spent most of his life at Lucca at the Chiesa della Madre di Dio, where he served as *Maestro di cappella.*[13]

The sonata, in the hand of copyist A, displays florid slow movements a partially figured bass, and numerous interpretive markings. The perpetual motion of the second and, less so, the fourth movements seems more idiomatic for the violin than the recorder.

## FERRONATI, GIACOMO

*Sonata [in fa magg.] à flauto solo, e basso*
I PAc. *Sinfonie* Mss. (CF-V-23), fols. 15r.-18r.

In the hand of copyist A, lacking the composer's first name; bass partially figured; few interpretive markings.

*Sinfonia [in sol min.] à flauto solo, é basso*
I PAc. *Sinfonie* MSS. (CF-V-23), fols. 19r.-22r.

In the hand of copyist B, bearing the composer's first and last names; bass partially figured. The perpetual motion and the passage work in the allegros, particularly the first one, suggest the violin rather than the recorder.

## FIOCCO, PIETRO ANTONIO

*Dix sonates pour les flûtes, dont il y en a VI à II flûtes de Mr. William Croft & IV à flûte & l basse [i.e., à l flûte & basse] de la composition de Mrs. Pepusch, Fioco & Pez.* — Amsterdam, E. Roger [1706].
2 parties in - 4, 13 pp., 10 pp.[14]
*Source:* **D-brd** JE

---

[13] See Schmidl, I, 287 together with the supplement (1938), p. 154; Eitner, II, 312; and Alberto Cavalli, "Canuti, Giovanni Antonio," *Die Musik in Geschichte und Gegenwart,* XV (1973), 1297.

[14] A literal quotation, excepting the additions in brackets, from *R.i.s.m.,* Series B, Vol. II: *Recueils imprimés du xviii$^e$ siècle,* p. 369. See also fn. 16, p. 26.

Pietro Antonio Fiocco, born in Venice ca. 1650 and having immigrated to Brussels in the 1680s, belonged to the first generation of a renowned family of Belgian musicians. After marrying in 1682, he acquired a position as assistant to the director (*lieutenant de la musique*) at the court and the church of Notre Dame du Sablon, finally in 1703 becoming the *maître,* a post that he held until his death in 1714. Although best known as a composer of church music, he composed a small number of instrumental works.[15]

The edition, preserved in a single copy in the Bibliothek des Marien-Gymnasiums at Jever (Germany), is unfortunately unavailable on microfilm at the present time. Sources enable one to determine merely that the collection was printed in 1706 and that it contains one, or perhaps two sonatas by Fiocco.[16] There is a possibility that some of the sonatas in the collection were taken from an earlier collection that was published in separate editions by John Young and by Walsh and Hare in 1700. The earlier collection is published by Walsh and Hare under the title, *Six Sonatas or Solos, Three for a Violin and Three for the Flute with a Thorough Bass for ye* [*the* in Young's edition] *Theorboe or Bass Viol. Composed by Mr. Wm. Crofts & an Italian Mr.*[17] The lack of complete ascriptions in these editions prevents further speculation about Fiocco's authorship.

### Sigr. GARZAROLI

*[VI] Suonate da camera à flauto è basso*
A Wn. Estense coll., No. 32. Ms. 16 pp.

*Suonata prima [in fa magg.]*

*Suonata 2a [in do magg.]*

*Suonata 3a [in sol min.]*

---

15 For more information about Pietro Antonio and his descendants, see Suzanne Clercx, "Fiocco," *Die Musik in Geschichte und Gegenwart,* IV (1955), 248-53 and Christiane Stellfeld, *Les Fiocco, une famille musiciens belges au xvii^e et xviii^e siècles,* Vol. VII of *Académie Royale de Belgique, Classe des Beaux-Arts, Mémoires,* Series II (Bruxelles: Palais des Académies, 1941).

16 See the reference cited in fn. 14 and compare Estienne Roger, "Catalogue des livres de musique nouvellement imprimez à Amsterdam chez Estienne Roger Marchand Libraire," appended to Jean François Félibien, *Recueil historique de la vie et des ouvrages des plus celebres architectes* (Amsterdam [1706]), [p. 9] and Lesure, *Bibliographie,* p. 87.

17 Copies of the two editions are preserved in a number of British libraries. See *The British Union Catalogue of Early Music Printed Before the Year 1801,* I (London: Butterworths Scientific Publications, 1957), 240.

*Suonata 4a [in re min.]*

*Suonata 5a [in sol magg.]*

*Suonata 6a [in si bem. magg.]*

The composer may be identical with, or related to Zach. Gazzarolli (Gazzaroli, Gazzaroll), an oboist who served in the *Hof- und Kammermusik* of Vienna from 1732-1759.[18]

The movements of these sonatas are short. The basses vary from unfigured to partially figured and there are few interpretive markings.

## GRANO, GIOVANNI BATTISTA

[VI] SOLOS / *for a* / GERMAN FLUTE / *a* HOBOY *or* VIOLIN / *with a* / *Thorough Bass for the* / HARPSICORD / *or* / BASS VIOLIN / *Compos'd by* / Iohn Baptist Grano. / / [advertisement follows] ... / / *London. Printed for and sold by I: Walsh servant to his Majesty at the Harp / and Hoboy in Catherine street in the Strand. and Ioseph Hare at the Viol / and Flute in Cornhill near the Royal Exchange.* [1728]

*Source:* **GB** Lbm (g. 422. j. (4.)) Title page and 24 pages of music

*Another copy:* **US** Wc (M 242 .G75 S6)

The publisher's imprint has been trimmed from the Library of Congress copy and the plate number 381 added, suggesting that the copy is a reprint of the early 1730s.[19]

Grano was a versatile musician who, beginning ca. 1714, gave concerts on the flute and the trumpet.[20] Some of his sonatas may therefore predate this edition ten years or more.

---

[18] See Ludwig von Köchel, *Die kaiserliche Hof-Musikkapelle zu Wien von 1543 bis 1867* (Vienna: Beck'sche Universitätsbuchhandlung, 1869), pp. 79, 84, and 87.

[19] See Smith and Humphries, *Walsh, 1721-1766*, p. 162.

[20] See Charles Burney, *A General History of Music*, IV (London: By the Author, 1789), 648 and also Michael Tilmouth, *A Calendar of References to Music in Newspapers Published in London and the Provinces, Royal Musical Association Research Chronicle No. 1* (1961), pp. 87 and 106.

## LOCATELLI, PIETRO
## Op. II

> XII / SONATE / à Flauto Traversiere Solo / è Basso. / *Dedicate* / AL
> MOLTO ILLUSTRE SIGNORE IL SIGNOR / NICOLA ROMSWINKEL /
> DI PIETRO LOCATELLI / da Bergamo / OPERA SECONDA. / *IN*
> *AMSTERDAM.* / *Apresso l'Autore f[lorins] 6* / *I: Morellon La*
> *Cave Sculp:* [1732]
>
> *Source:* **GB** Lcm (II. B. 16. (1.) )  Title page bearing the composer's signature,
> dedication, 49 pages of music, and privilege dating 1731.
>
> *Other copies:* **GB** Lbm (g. 294. b.) signed P.° Locatelli and lacking a privilege,
> Ob; **NL** Lu two different editions, one including the privilege of 1731, the
> other including a privilege dating 1752; **S** Skma, SK including the privilege of
> 1731; **US** NH

After his early studies with Corelli, his travels and performances in England and
on the Continent, and his service at Dresden, Locatelli settled in Amsterdam
in 1729.  In 1731 he obtained a privilege to print and publish his compositions
in the States of Holland and West-Vriesland.  Thus, beginning in 1732 with his
second opus, Locatelli published the greater part of his nine opuses of sonatas
and concertos himself.[21]

The flute sonatas were advertised well in advance of their publication.  On
August 10, 1731, the following subscription announcement appeared:

> Pierre Locatelli demeurant à Amsterdam, avertit le public que
> conformément à l'Octroi qu'il a obtenue de N. S. les Etats de
> Holland & de West Frise & daté du 24 juillet 1731, il fera imprimer
> Douze Sonates a Flauto Traversiere solo & Basso & tous les autres
> ouvrages.  On peut en attendant souscrire pour les dits Sonates a
> Flauto Traversiere chez l'Auteur où l'on en trouve les conditions.
> Cet ouvrage sera l'opera seconda.

On the next day the same announcement, printed in Dutch, appeared in the
*Amsterdamsche Courant.*  The edition was advertised, apparently for the first
time, on May 10 of the following year in the same paper.[22]

---

[21] Whether or not Locatelli played the flute is unknown.  An inventory of his estate
shows, however, that he owned two transverse flutes and a *flute d'amour, i.e.,* a flute in *a*.
For more biographical information and a thematic catalog, see Arend J. Koole, *Pietro
Antonio Locatelli da Bergamo* (Amsterdam: Jasonpers, 1949).  Supplementary information,
including a revised list of works and sources, both printed and manuscript, appears in Albert
Dunning and Arend Koole, "Pietro Antonio Locatelli, Nieuwe bijdragen tot de kennis van
zijn leven en werken," *Tijdschrift van de Vereniging voor Nederlandse Muziekgeschiedenis,*
XX/nos. 1-2 (1964-1965), 52-96.

[22] See Koole, *Locatelli,* pp. 49-50.

The work was dedicated to Nicola Romswinkel (1708-1755), a town councilman at Leiden and a pupil of the composer.[23] The dedication reads:

Molto illustre Signore.

Le singolari qualità di V. S. Molt' illustre, accompagnate dalle infinite obligazioni, che le professo, mi hanno conciliato una sì grande stima, ed un così vero rispetto verso la di lei stimatissima Persona, che ho desiderato è già lungo tempo di poterlene dar qualche picciola dimostrazione in contrasegno della mia ossequiosa servitù. Non avendone però incontrato mai fin'ad ora occasione più favorevole, son costretto a prevalermi di questa, che mi si porge presentemente nel mandare alla luce queste picciole Sonate, pregandola di voler benignamente accordarmi la grazia di poterle publicare sotto la di lei Protezzione, sapendo io di sicuro, che non solamente saranno benissimo appoggiate, ma anche che dovevo con tutta giustizia indrizzarle a V. S. percioche si è degnata farmi l'onore di voler esser mio discepolo, e servirsi delle mie povere istruzzioni non per altro che per conservar in lei quell' affezzione, che sempre ha avuta per quest' Arte liberale. Prenda ella dunque, e gradisca queste Musicali mie Composizioni, che con animo affatto sincero prendo la libertà di dedicarle, affinche, vedendo che V. S. si compiace d'accoglierle benignamente, possa io lusingarmi d'averle in qualche maniera spiegato il vero desiderio, che ho di dimostrarle la mia gratitudine, e d'onorare insieme le mie Stampe col di lei Nome, mentre con i più vivi, e sinceri sentimenti dell' animo mio mi pregio d'esser con tutta la stima, ed ossequio di V. S. molto illustre.

> Devotisso. ed Obblgo.
> Servo
> Pietro Locatelli.

Finely engraved by Morellon, the edition closely resembles some of those issued by Le Cène who, incidentally, listed the work in his catalog of 1737.[24]

---

[23] It is perhaps more than a coincidence that Locatelli's edition appeared just ten days before Romswinkel's marriage. See Koole, *Locatelli,* p. 50.

[24] Michel-Charles Le Cène, *Catalogue des livres de musique imprimés à Amsterdam, chez Michel Charles Le Cène* (Amsterdam [1737]; Gemeentemuseum, Scheurleer Collection, 4 B 59), p. 35. The edition must have been sold by numerous dealers throughout Europe. See two catalogs by the Augsburg publisher, Jacob Lotter, the Younger (1726-1804), *Catalogus aller musikalische Bücher* (1753), facsim. ed., ed. Adolph Layer, Vol. II of *Catalogus musicus* (Kassel: Bärenreiter, 1964), p. 19 and *Musikalischer Catalogus aller derjenigen Bücher und Musicalien* (Augsburg: 1773; Brit. Mus., Hirsch IV. 1108. a.), p. 28.

## LOCATELLI, PIETRO
## Other Editions

SOLOS / *for a* / GERMAN FLUTE / *or* / VIOLIN / *with a Thorough Bass for the* / HARPSICORD *or* BASS VIOLIN / *Compos'd by* / PIETRO LOCATELLI. / *Opera Seconda. / /* [lengthy advertisement follows] *... London. Printed for and Sold by* I. Walsh, *Musick Printer, and* / *Instrument maker to his Majesty, at the Harp and Hoboy in Cathe-/rine Street in the Strand.* No. 603 [1737]

*Source:* GB Lbm (g. 280. i. (5.) ) Title page and 25 pages of music numbered as pages 2-27. Contains Sonatas II, I, IX, X, IV, and VII.

*Other copies:* GB Ckc two copies, one with the plate number (Rw. 16. 49 (1) ) and the other without it, Er, Ob; I BGi without the plate number; US Wc (M 291 .L81 Op. 2W) [25]

XII / SONATE / *à Flauto Traversiere solo* / è Basso / DI PIETRO LOCATELLI / DA BERGAMO. / *Opera Secunda* / *NOUVELLE EDITION* / *Prix 8ʰ/* Gravées par le Sʳ Hüe. / *Chez Mʳ LeClerc le cadet rüe Sᵗ Honoré à la Ville* / *de Constantinople près L'Oratoire.* / *Le Sʳ LeClerc Mᵈ rüe du Roule à la Croix d'or.* / *Mᵐᵉ Boivin Mᵈᵉ rüe Sᵗ Honoré à la regle d'or.* / *AVEC PRIVILEGE DU ROY.* / Bourgoin Scripcit [1737?] [26]

*Source:* B Bc (S 12,216) Title page, catalog, and 49 pages of music numbered as pages 2-50. The format indicates that the edition was copied from Locatelli's first edition.

*Other copies:* B Bc (S 5573) including a later catalog; F Pc 2 copies; US R, Wc (M 242 .L) of which the title page is altered by the removal of Bourgoin's name and the changing of C. N. (le Sr.) LeClerc's address. In addition, a later catalog of Jean (le cadet) LeClerc is included.

Locatelli's flute sonatas were advertised widely by other publishers. They are listed, for example, in Le Cêne's catalog of 1737, John Cox's catalog of ca. 1751, Johnson's catalog of ca. 1754, Peter Thompson's catalog of ca. 1752, and Jacob

---

[25] Koole claims that other copies are found in the Istituto musicale "Donizetti" in Bergamo and the Royal College of Music, London. See Koole, *Locatelli,* p. 276. I have no information about the first; as for the second, Koole may have been referring to a copy of the first edition. See page 28 in the present study.

[26] The edition is advertised in J. LeClerc's *Catalogue* of 1737, p. 57. A fifteen year privilege to one of the LeClercs was announced on November 27, 1738, according to George Cucūel, "Quelques documents sur la librairie musicale au xviiiᵉ siècle," *Sammelbände der Internationalen Musikgesellschaft,* XIII (1911-1912), 387. A date of ca. 1736 is suggested in Dunning and Koole, p. 77.

Lotter's catalogs of 1753 and 1773. It is doubtful that these men issued their own editions, however. Le Cêne and Lotter apparently sold the first edition. Cox, Johnson, and Thompson probably sold the one published by Walsh.[27]


**Manuscripts**[28]

> *XII Sonate a flauto traverso con cembalo di Locatelli*
> **A Wn.** Ms. 15564

Formerly owned by the composer, Johann Gottfried Schicht (1753-1823), whose last name appears on the outside title page. 92 pages plus separate title pages for all of the sonatas. Contains twelve sonatas in the original order.

> *[XI Sonatas for Flauto Traverso and Bass]*
> **D-brd** B-MG. Ms. 13061/5

Includes Sonatas I-VII and IX-XII.

> *[IX Sonates for Flauto Traverso and Bass]*
> **F Pc.** Ms. L. 10,649

Intermixed with works by other composers. Included are Sonatas I, II—lacking the third movement, III, V-VIII, X—lacking the third movement, and XI. 33 pages of music.

> *[Three Sonatas for Flauto Traverso and Bass]*
> **D-ddr** SW1. Mss. 3444-46

Separate title pages and 18 pages of music. Containing Sonatas IV, III—transposed from B♭ major to C major, and XI—first movement incomplete.

---

[27] See Le Cêne, *Catalogue* of 1737, p. 35; John Cox, "A Catalogue of Vocal and Instrumental Music," appended to Felice Giardini, *Sei Sonate di cembalo con violino o flauto traverso,* Opera terza (London [ca. 1751]; Brit. Mus., Hirsch III. 225), [p. 1]; Johnson, "Catalogue" of ca. 1754, [p. 1]; Peter Thompson, "A Catalogue of Musick" (London [ca. 1752]; Brit. Mus., Hirsch IV. 1111. (14.)), [p. 1]; and Lotter, *Catalogus* of 1753, p. 19 and *Catalogus* of 1773, p. 28. Le Cêne's catalog does not give a plate number. Lotter's catalogs indicate an edition that was published in Amsterdam. Both publishers indicate a price of six florins.

[28] Minor sources have been omitted. For additional sources, including arrangements and keyboard transcriptions, see Dunning and Koole, pp. 77-78.

MARCELLO, BENEDETTO
Op. II ̃

[XII] SVONATE / A FLAVTO SOLO / Con il suo Basso Continuo per Violoncello ò Cembalo / DI / BENEDETTO MARCELLO / NOBILE VENETO / *DILETTANTE DI CONTRAPVNTO* / E / ACCADEMICO FILARMONICO / ET / ARCADE / OPERA SECONDA: / / IN VENETIA Da Gioseppe Sala. MDCCXII. / Si Vendono à S: Gio: Grisottimo. All' Insegna del Rè David. CON LICENZA DE SVPERIORI. [obl. fol. printed from movable type]

*Source:* I Bc (GG. 135)   Title page and 73 pages of music

*Another copy:* D-brd WD

A facsimile of the title page is printed in the first volume of a complete, modern edition, identified on page 53.

**Second Edition**

XII SUONATE / A FLAUTO SOLO / Con il suo Basso Continuo per Violoncello ò Cembalo, / DI / BENEDETTO MARCELLO / NOBILE VENETO, / Dillettante di Contrapunto, e Accademico / Filarmonico, et Arcade / OPERA SECONDA / A AMSTERDAM / Chez Estienne Roger Marchand Libraire / *Nº 368* [1715]

*Source:* DK Kk (H. & F. Rungs Musik Archiv No. 508)   Title page and 36 pages of music numbered as pages 2-37.

*Other copies:* D-brd WD; D-ddr Bds; US Wc (M 242 .M25 Op. 2)

**Another Edition**

XII / SOLOS / *for a* / GERMAN FLUTE / *or* / VIOLIN / *with a Thorough Bass for the* / HARPSICORD / *or* / BASS VIOLIN / *Compos'd by* / Sig.ʳ *Benneditti Marcello.* / *Opera Primo.* / / *London. Printed for and sold by* I: Walsh *Musick Printer & Instrument maker* / *to his Majesty at the Harp and Hoboy in Catherine Street in the Strand.* / Nº 419 [1732]

*Source:* GB Lbm (g. 1008)   Title page and 46 pages of music

*Other copies:* I BGi; US NH, Wc (M 242 .M) lacking the plate number and therefore probably from an earlier printing.

The sonatas are reordered and in some cases transposed to better suit the transverse flute as shown below.

| Original | | Present |
| --- | --- | --- |
| Number | Key | Key |
| I | F | D |
| IV | e | d |
| IX | C | C |
| II | d | b |
| III | g | e |
| VII | B♭ | B♭ |
| VI | C | G |
| XII | F | F |
| VIII | d | b |
| XI | g | e |
| X | a | a |
| V | G | G |

Marcello's sonatas were also sold, although probably not printed by John Johnson.[29]

### OGLIO, DOMENICO DALL'

A man whose biographical details remain largely unknown, Dall'Oglio was born ca. 1700, apparently in Padua, and died at Narva (Estonia) in 1764. Together with a younger brother, Giuseppe (dates unknown), Domenico served the greater part of his life at the Russian court at St. Petersburg, beginning about 1735. Much later, in 1762, the year Catherine the Great (1729-1796) ascended the throne, he apparently became concertmaster. Domenico's achievement as a composer is yet to be determined from a large body of scattered manuscripts and printed editions.[30]

Among the many works ascribed to the composer are two solo flute sonatas that were apparently first published in a collection by Gerhard Fredrik Witvogel in Amsterdam. The collection, of which there is no known copy, is listed in Witvogel's catalog of 1746 as:

---

[29] See Johnson, *Catalogue* of ca. 1754, [p. 1].

[30] For more information about the composer, see Albert Mell, "Dall' Oglio," *Die Musik in Geschichte und Gegenwart,* IX (1961), 1913-16.

80. *6 Sonate a flauto traversa solo e Violoncello o Basso Continuo d'Alcu[n]i Famosi Maestri Comme di Jean Fredrick Groneman. Domenico Dall'Oglio, e Giuseppe san Martini, libro secondo.* 61 Exemp. [pp.] f[lorins] 3:— [31]

The plate number 80 suggests that the collection was published ca. 1740.

**OGLIO, DOMENICO DALL'**
**Later Editions**

VI SONATE / a Flauto Traversa solo, e / Violoncello o Basso Continuo / *d'Alcuni famosi Maestri* / *Comme di* / JEAN FREDRIK GRONEMAN, / DOMENICO DALL' OGLIO, / GIUSEPPE SAN MARTINI. / / . . . London Printed & Sold by *John Cox* at the Bass Viol & Flute, in Sweetings Alley opposite the / East Door of the Royal Exchange, late *M.ʳ John Simpson's,* / where may be had [lengthy advertisement follows] . . . [ca. 1762]

*Source:* **GB** CDp (34FG?)  Title page and 34 pages of music

*Another copy:* **NL** DHgm

The collection includes two sonatas by Dall' Oglio, one in D minor (No. II) and one in G major (No. V). The edition was apparently sold also by Johnson and Bremner. Breitkopf and Härtel offered the same collection in its catalog supplement of 1779-1780.[32]

---

[31] Gerhard Fredrik Witvogel, *Catalogus van een uitmuntende verzameling van een groote extra fraaije gedrukte partye exemplaren van nieuw musicq* (Amsterdam: Arent Rampen, 1746; Gemeentemuseum, Scheurleer Collection), p. 9. See also Albert Dunning, *De muziekuitgever Gerhard Fredrik Witvogel en zijn fonds,* Vol. II of *Muziekhistorische Monografieën,* published by the Vereniging voor Nederlandse Muziekgeschiedenis (Utrecht: A. Oosthoek, 1966), p. 52.

[32] See Johnson, *Catalogue* of ca. 1754, [p. 1]; Bremner, *Catalogue* of 1782, p. 2; and Breitkopf und Härtel, *The Breitkopf Thematic Catalogue, 1762-1787,* facsim. ed., ed. Barry S. Brook (New York: Dover, 1966), Supplement XIII (1799-1780), 16.

## PLATTI, GIOVANNI
## Op. III

*SEI SONATE / a Flauto Traversiere Solo con Violoncello overo*
*Cembalo. / Dedicate / / All'Illustrissimo e Reverendissimo Signore*
*Il Signor / PIETRO FILIPPO DI KRVFFT, / Scolastico e Canonico*
*della Collegiata di Santo Cuniberto in Colonia. / Composte dà /*
*Giovanni Platti, Virtuoso di Camera di Sua Altezza Reverendissima,*
*/ MONSIGNOR FEDERICO CARLO, / Prencipe del Sacro Romano*
*Impero, e Vescovo di Bamberga / e Wirzburgo, Duca di Franconia,*
*&c. &c. / OPERA TERZA. / Alle Spese di Giovanni Vlrico Haffner,*
*Virtuoso di Liuto in Norimberga. / N.ͬo VI. Stor fecit.* [obl. fol. 1743?]

Source: **D-brd** Mbs (1176)   Title page, dedication, and 33 pages of music

*Other copies:* **D-brd** Mbs imperfect second copy; **D-ddr** LEm; **GB** Lbm

Platti, born ca. 1700 in Venice, spent most of his life at the court of Würzburg where
he died in 1763. He served there under the *Kapellmeister,* Fortunato Chelleri
(1690-1757), with whom he probably immigrated about 1722. Platti was a versatile
singer, a virtuoso on the oboe and violin,[33] and, very probably, a harpsichordist.

There is good reason to believe that he and Quantz were acquaintances, for
Quantz mentions a visit that he made to Würzburg in October, 1723, where he
performed on the flute for Bishop von Schönborn, who apparently offered him
a position. Quantz also mentions Chelleri, reports that the *Kapelle* consisted
of some twenty persons, and claims that the meeting had been arranged through
the intercession of one of his friends (Platti?).[34]

Platti's compositions include four printed opuses of instrumental works issued
by the Nürnburg composer-publisher, Johann Ulrich Haffner (1711-1767) and
a large number of manuscripts.[35] His flute sonatas were published during his
service to Prince-Bishop Friedrich Karl von Schönborn (reigned 1729-1743),
as indicated on the title page. Executed by Johann Wilhelm Stör (1705-1760)
ca. 1743 [36] the engraving of the title page, dedication, and music is very fine.

---

[33] Ernst Ludwig Gerber, *Historisch-biographisches Lexicon der Tonkünstler,* II (Leipzig:
J. G. I. Breitkopf, 1792), 159.

[34] See Johann Joachim Quantz, "Herrn Johann Joachim Quantzens Lebenslauf, von
ihm selbst entworfen," published in Friedrich Wilhelm Marpurg, *Historisch-kritische*
*Beyträge zur Aufnahme der Musik,* I (Berlin: Johann Jacob Schuetzens sel. Wittwe, 1755),
221-22 or the translation in Paul Nettl, *Forgotten Musicians* (New York: Philosophical
Library, 1951), p. 298.

[35] For more information about the composer see Lothar Hoffmann-Erbrecht, "Platti,
Giovanni Benedetto," *Die Musik in Geschichte und Gegenwart,* X (1962), 1341-42.

[36] See Lothar Hoffmann-Erbrecht, "Der Nürnburger Musikverlager Johann Ulrich
Haffner," *Acta Musicologica,* XXVI (1954), 116 and 119.

The dedication to Kruftt, an amateur flutist, reads:

ILLUSTRISSIMO E REVERENDISSIMO SIGNORE.

Le rare virtù, che risplendono nella degnissima persona di V. S. Illma., unite a tante altre qualità particolari, che fanno l'ammirazione di tutti quelli, che hanno la capacità di poter stimarne il gran valore; mi spronano à non slontanarmi in cercar protezione altrove per questo qualsisia picciolo parto mio, che si presenta a gl'occhi di V. S. Illma., à chi solo resterà umilmente consacrato: supplicandola divotissimamente di riguardarlo come un sicurissimo pegno della grandissima stima, ch'io faccio de'Suoi meriti assai cospicui, e della venerazione distinta che per sempre LE porterò. Queste sei sonate sono state composte per far particolare piacere à quei che si dilettano del Flauto Traversiere. V. S. Illma., (di cui fò gloria d'esser fin adesso nel tempo del SUO Soggiorno in Wirzburgo, l'indegno suo maestro sopra questo dolcissimo stromento) è tanto avanzata nella teorica e nella prattica di esso, ch'ELLA fà rossore non solamente ai dilettanti, mà ancora ai professori medemi. Nissuno dunque potrà giudicare meglio di questa mia debole fatica, che V. S. Illma., sotto gli auspizii di cui io hò l'ardire di publicarla, lusingandomi per certo, ch'ella sarà fuori d'ogni censura d'un Zoilo, pur ch'ella abbia la SUA approvazione. Onde si degni di volgere qualche benigno sguardo a queste mie rozze note, che sodisfatto appieno sarò nelle mie brame, lequali non hanno altra mira che quella di poter protestarmi per sempre con tutto l'ossequio.

di V. S. Illma. e Reverendma.

In Wirzburgo.          umilissimo e divotissimo Servo
                       Giovanni Platti.

Documents reveal that the edition was sold by the Viennese firm of Peter Conrad Monath (1683-1747) and also Lotter in Augsburg who advertised it as late as 1773. Both merchants priced the edition at 1 florin 45 *Kreuzer*.[37]

A copy of the work belonging to the Badische Landesbibliothek (formerly the Grossherzogliche Bibliothek) at Karlsruhe[38] was destroyed during World War II.

**ROSA, FILIPPO**

*Sinfonia [in fa magg.] à flauto solo, e basso*
I PAc. *Sinfonie* Mss. (CF-V-23), fols. 23r.-26r.

---

[37] See Hannelore Gericke, *Der Wiener Musikalienhandel von 1700 bis 1778,* Vol. V of *Wiener musikwissenschaftliche Beiträge* (Graz: H. Böhlaus Nachf., 1960), p. 42; Lotter's *Catalogus* of 1753, pp. 19 and 38 and his *Catalogus* of 1773, pp. 28 and 55.

[38] Listed in Eitner, VII, 471.

In the hand of copyist B; bass unfigured; the work displays florid treatment and numerous interpretive markings in the "Grave" and perpetual motion in the final "Allegro."

## SAMMARTINI, GIUSEPPE
## Op. I

[XII] SONATE / *à Solo, et a due Flauti Trauersi* / *col Loro Basso* / OPERA PRIMA / Dedicata / *al* / *ALTEZZA REALE* / *di* / FEDRICO / *PRINCIPE DI VALLIA* / *ET ELETTORALE DI BRVNSVIK* / DA GIUSEPPE SAN MARTINI / *Milanese* / *A AMSTERDAM* / *Chez* MICHEL CHARLES LE CENE [Plate No. 583. 1736]

*Source:* **GB** Lk (R.M. 16. e. 26.) [*Parte primo*], trios printed in three separate parts each with a title page and a dedication—*Flauto traversiere primo* with 14 pages of music bearing the plate number 583 on the *recto* side of each folio, *Flauto traversiere secondo* with 12 pages of music, *Basso* with 13 pages of music; *Parte secondo,* solo sonatas in score, lacing a title page and a dedication, with 29 pages of music.

Le Cène's edition also appears with two other title pages. One of them, which suggests that the edition was printed primarily for the composer, reads:

SONATE / *à Solo, et a due Flauti Trauersi* / *col Loro Basso* / OPERA PRIMA / Dedicata / *al* / *ALTEZZA REALE* / *di* / FEDERICO / *PRINCIPE DI VALLIA* / *ET ELETTORALE DI BRVNSVIK* / DI GIUSEPPE SAN MARTINI / *Milanese* / *LONDON Printed for the Author* [1736]

*Copies:* **B** Bc solos only (S 5587); **GB** Ckc trios (Rw. 23. 53/55) and solos (Rw. L¹. 3. 12*); Lbm trios (g. 274. h. (5.) ) and solos (g. 86. b.); **US** NYp trios *Flauto primo* only, Wc (M 317 .S19 Op. 1 (B) )

The copy of the trios in the Rowe Music Library of Kings College (Rw. 23. 53/55) contains a privilege granting to Sammartini sole printing and publishing rights in the British Empire for a period of fourteen years, extending from the privilege date of June 10, 1736.[39]

39 This information eliminates some, but not all of the confusion about Giuseppe's first opus. In Henry G. Mishkin, "The Published Instrumental Works of Giovanni Battista Sammartini: A Bibliographical Reappraisal," *The Musical Quarterly,* XLV/no. 3 (July 1959), 363-64 and the *British Union-Catalogue,* II, 920, one finds references to a collection of duets for two flutes published as Giuseppe's first opus by James Oswald in 1750. A similar work is advertised by Walsh in a catalog of ca. 1731 (see Smith and Humphries, *Walsh, 1721-1766,* p. 12, item 11d) and in a catalog of flute music dating ca. 1733 (see p. 10 including fn. 2). Other uncertainty concerns "Six Sonatas for Two Flutes and a Base," a work that Charles Burney claims in his *History,* IV, 650, was Giuseppe's first English publication, advertised October 6, 1927. Could the latter be an early edition of trio sonatas for violins that Mishkin states (p. 363) are by Giovanni Battista, or another work?

The third title page reads:

SIX SONATES / À UNE FLÛTE TRAVERSIERE / auec la Basse, / *et six* / *TRIO A DEUX FLÛTES* / *Avec la Basse.* / PAR M.ᴿ JOSEPH S.ᵀ MARTINI / Milanois. / *Premier Ouvrâge* / DEDIÉ / *A. S. A. R.* / *Le Prince De Galles.* / / Gravé à Paris. / *Denise Vincent. Scrip.*

*Copy:* **B** Bc trios only (V 13,437)

The edition was probably supplied to Paris publishers by Le Cène.

Sammartini's dedication, which in its engraved format resembles a title page, reads:

FREDERICO / *Regio Walliae* / *Electorali Brunsuici* / *PRINCIPI* / *Munifico Artium omnium* / PATRONO / *Haec qualiacunque Musicae* / *Tentamenta* / *Gratum* / *Obsequi et Observantiae* / *Testimonium* / D. D. D. / *Devotus et humillimus Cliens* / *Joseph Santus Martinus* / Londini. / MD.CC.XXXVI.

## SAMMARTINI, GIUSEPPE
## Op. I, Other Editions

[PART II] VI / SONATE / A Flauti Traversi Solo / col Loro Basso. / DEDICATA / *al* / ALTEZZA REALE / *di* / FREDERICO / *Principe di Wallia* / *Et Elettorale di Brunswik.* / *da* / GIUSEPPE SAN MARTINI. / MILANESE. / OPERA PRIMA. / Gravé par Labassée. / Prix 4ᵗᵗ 10.ᶠ / A PARIS / CHEZ M.ʳ LeClerc le Cadet rue S.ᵗ Honorè *vis à vis l'Oratoire* / *à la Ville de Constantinople.* / *Le S.ʳ LeClerc Marchand rue du Roule a la Croix d'Or.* / *Madame Boivin Marchande rue S.ᵗ Honoré à la Règle d'Or.* / *Avec Privilege du Roy.* [ca. 1740]

*Source:* **GB** Ckc (Rw. 16. 47. (5) ) Title page, catalog, and 31 pages of music

*Another copy:* **I** G1 (A. 3. 48. (N. 2. 48.) ) identified as "OPERA Terza," lacking the second line of the above imprint, and containing a different catalog.

[PART II] *Giuseppe San Martini Milaneese Opera prima Libro Secondo 6 Sonate a flaute Traversiere solo e Basso Continuo* [Amsterdam, Gerhard Fredrik Witvogel] 32 Exemp. [pp.] — f[lorins] 2:10 [No. 91. 1742 or 1743].[40]

---

[40] Listed in Witvogel, *Catalogus* of 1746, p. 9.

[Part II] *SIX* / SOLOS / for a / GERMAN FLUTE / or / VIOLIN /
*with a Through Bass for the* / HARPSICORD or VIOLONCELLO /
COMPOS'D BY / GIUSEPPE S. MARTINI / of LONDON. / OPERA
XII. / / London. *Printed for* I. Walsh *in Catharine Street in* $\overset{e}{y}$
*Strand* / [lengthy advertisement follows] . . . [1757]

*Source:* **GB** Lbm (g. 86. g.)  Title page and 28 pages of music

*Another copy:* **GB** Ckc (Rw. 16. 62 (8) )

## SAMMARTINI, GIUSEPPE
## Op. II

XII SONATE / *a Flauto Traversiere Solo* / *Con il Basso* / OPERA
SECONDA / *DI* / GIUSEPPE SAN MARTINI / *Milanese* / *A* /
*AMSTERDAM* / *Chez* MICHEL CHARLES LE CENE / N.º 584. [1736?]

*Source:* **GB** Lbm (g. 86. f.)  Title page and 58 pages of music

Notice that the plate number is consecutive to that of Sammartini's first opus.
It is curious that the edition lacks a dedication to the Prince of Wales and that
no copies printed for the composer have been found.

## Other Editions

[Nos. I-VI] *SIX* / SOLOS / For a / GERMAN FLUTE or VIOLIN / with
a THOROUGH BASS  for the / HARPSICORD or VIOLONCELLO /
COMPOS'D BY / *SIG.ᴿ GIUSEPPE S.ᵀ MARTINI* / *Opera 2ª* / London.
*Printed for* I. Walsh *in Catharine Street in the Strand* / [lengthy
advertisement follows] . . . [ca. 1745]

*Source:* **GB** Lbm (g. 422. b. (6.) )  Title page and 29 pages of music

*Another issue:* **GB** T with *2ª* written out as "Seconda" [1745]; **US** AA
(M 242 .S19 1745) with "Seconda" added and lacking the last line of the
above advertisement (and price).

[Nos. VII-XII] *SIX* / SOLOS / For a / GERMAN FLUTE or VIOLIN /
with a THOROUGH BASS for the / HARPSICORD or VIOLONCELLO
/ COMPOS'D BY / SIG.ᴿ GIUSEPPE S.ᵀ MARTINI / *Opera Quarta.* /
London. *Printed for* I. Walsh *in Catharine Street in the Strand* /
[lengthy advertisement follows] . . . [ca. 1747]

*Source:* **GB** Lbm (g. 422. b. (7.) )  Title page and 26 pages of music numbered
as pages 2-28, Ob.

The title page is printed from the same plate used for the preceding edition; only the opus number is changed. Sammartini's sonatas were advertised by many other London publishers. The fact that some of them list a set of sonatas identified as Opus IV suggests that they sold Walsh's editions.

**SAMMARTINI, GIUSEPPE**
**Op. XIII**

> *Six / SOLOS /* For a / *GERMAN FLUTE /* VIOLIN or HAUTBOY /
> *with a / Thorough Bass. /* Composed by / *Sigʳ Giuseppe Sᵗ Martini*
> / Op. XIII. / / LONDON Printed for *John Johnson* opposite Bow
> Church in Cheapside [lengthy advertisement follows] . . . [1760?]
>
> *Source:* **GB** Lbm (g. 422. b. (8.)) Title page and 24 pages of music
>
> *Other copies:* **GB** Lbm (g. 422. g. (4.)), Mp

The collection is advertised by Johnson in a catalog of 1770 at a price of three shillings.[41]

**Other Published Sonatas**

Another sonata by the composer appeared in the collection of Witvogel, identified and described under the name of Dall' Oglio on page 34. In later editions of the collection the composition, in G major, is placed third (see p. 34).

An additional sonata that requires consideration is found in a collection entitled:

> *SIX /* SOLOS / for a / GERMAN FLUTE OR VIOLIN / *with a Thorough*
> *Bass for the /* HARPSICORD or VIOLONCELLO / *Compos'd by / SIGʳ*
> *FRANCESCO XAVEᵒ RICHTER &c.* / / LONDON. *Printed for* I. Walsh *in*
> *Catharine Street in the Strand. /* [lengthy advertisement follows] . . . [1764]
>
> *Source:* **GB** Lk (R.M. 17. f. 20. (6.)) Title page and 28 pages of music
>
> *Other copies:* **GB** Lbm (g. 71. f. (3.)), LEp

---

[41] John Johnson, "A Catalogue of Vocal and Instrumental Music, 1770, Printed and Sold by John Johnson, at the Harp and Crown in Cheapside, London." (Brit. Mus., Hirsch IV. 1111. (10.)), [p. 1].

The sonata, in D major, is second in the collection. The work cannot be ascribed definitely to Giuseppe, however, for the first name of the composer is missing. Moreover, the composer is identified as "St. Martini of Milan," a name that frequently indicated G. B. Sammartini as opposed to Giuseppe of London.[42] The composer may someday be determined after the Sammartinis have received more study.

**Works in Manuscript**

> *[XVII] Sinfonie di Giuseppe S. Martino*
> I PAc. Ms. CF-V-20. 70 fols.

A volume of solo sonatas of which nine are called sonatas, seven bear the name *sinfonia*, and one is entitled a concerto. The works are in the hand of copyist A, the primary contributor to Ms. CF-V-23 (see pp. 16 and 21), and possess unfigured basses. The number of errors and inconsistencies in notation and the attribution "Del S: Martino" rule out the possibility that copyist A might be Sammartini himself.

Because the manuscript is in the hand of a copyist, there is some question about the authenticity of the entire collection. One can be reasonably certain that at least some of the works are by the composer, however. Evidence of this is found in the identical and similar works preserved in another manuscript collection bearing Giuseppe's name in the Sibley Library (see p. 42). Moreover, the first movement of the third recorder sonata, also in F major, is nearly identical with the second movement of the seventh flute sonata in Op. II; and a pair of minuets that concludes this recorder sonata are similar to the pair that concludes the flute sonata, although the second minuet of the latter is much longer. Certain internal traits suggest, moreover, that the manuscript collection may include sonatas written during the composer's early years in Italy, before he left in the late 1720s for London.[43]

---

[42] See Smith and Humphries, *Walsh, 1721-1766*, pp. 291 ff.
[43] See McGowan, pp. 356 ff.

## SAMMARTINI, GIUSEPPE
## Works in Manuscript

*[XXVII] Sonatas for Flute or Oboe & Basso Continuo*
**US R. MS. M 241 .S189. 228 pp.**

A volume of solo sonatas, beginning with six for oboe, compiled from the work of two primary and several other copyists. Contrary to the title, the collection contains one work specifically designated for the violin and attributed to Giambattista Sammartini (Sonata [XXVII], pp. 221-27), plus three other works that, judging from multiple stops and extensive across-the-strings figuration, must also have been intended for the violin (Sonatas [VII], [XII], and [XX], pp. 61-67, 101-7, and 165-71). In addition, a three-voiced "Rond[e] au" has been erroneously bound within the pages of an oboe sonata (No. [VI]). The works of primary interest in this study, therefore, are four sonatas designated for the *traversa* (Nos. [VIII-XI], pp. 69 ff.) and thirteen works designated for recorder (Nos. [XIII]-[XIX] and [XXI]-[XXVI], pp. 109 ff.).

The great majority of sonatas in the collection are cast in three movements, suggesting a relatively late period in the composer's life. Actually, however, the collection includes a number of sonatas that are identical with or similar to works preserved in the manuscript at Parma and also Opus II (see pp. 39-41) as shown below.

| *[XXVII] Sonatas* US R | *Other Sources* |
|---|---|
| *Sonata [I] à oboe solo*<br>(C major) | *[XVII] Sinfonie,* I PAc [XII]<br>(F major) |
| *Sonata [X] à fluta traversier*<br>(D major, pp. 85-91) | *[XVII] Sinfonie* [VI]<br>(F major) |
| *Sonata [XI] à fluta traversier*<br>(G major, pp. 93-99) | *[XVII] Sinfonie* [VII]<br>(G major) |
| *Sonata [XIII] à flauto solo*<br>(G minor, pp. 109-15)<br>Lacking the first movement of the<br>other version and containing another<br>adagio as the second movement | Op. II, No. VIII<br>(E minor) |
| *Sonata [XXIII] à flauto solo*<br>(F major, pp. 189-95)<br>In four movements, containing an<br>added second movement | Op. II, No. II<br>(C major) |
| *Sonata [XXVI] à flauto solo*<br>(F major, pp. 213-20)<br>Lacking a fourth movement | *[XVII] Sinfonie* [II]<br>(F major) |

**SANTINI, ALLESSANDRO**

*6 Sonate à flauto e basso*
I Vqs. Ms. Cl. VIII, Cod. 29, pp. 1-27

*Sonata prima [in fa magg.]*

*Sonata seconda [in re min.]*

*Sonata terza [in do magg.]*

*Sonata quarta [in sol magg.]*

*Sonata quinta [in re min.]*

*Sonata sesta [in fa magg.]*

The basses are unfigured and there are numerous interpretive markings, especially slurred patterns. The collection includes the *flauto primo* part for four additional sonatas, probably trio sonatas (last eight pages).

**SANTIS, GIOVANNI de**
**Op. IV**

XII SONATA / à Flauto Traversiere o Violino Solo / è Basso Continuo o Violoncello / *di* / GIOVANNI DE SANTIS / NAPOLITANO. / Opera Quarta. / / *Stampate a Spese / di* / GERHARD FREDRIK WITVOGEL, / *Organista del Tempio Nuovo Luterano* / A AMSTERDAM. / Nº 32. [ca. 1734]

*Source:* Leufsta Castle, Sweden. Collection of Baron Carl de Geer. Title page and 56 pages of music

Giovanni de Santis was a Neopolitan violinist who, in addition to composing twelve flute sonatas, wrote solo sonatas, *divertimenti,* and concertos for the violin, and also two operas. Although his dates are unknown, Walther reports that the man came into prominence in the early 1730s.[44] All of his known instrumental works were published before the middle of the century, established

---

[44] Johann Gottfried Walther, *Musicalisches Lexicon,* facsim. of the original ed. of 1732, ed. Richard Schaal, Vol. III of *Documenta musicologica,* Series I (Kassel: Bärenreiter, 1953), 541.

by the fact that they are listed in Witvogel's catalog of 1746.[45] Writers generally claim that Witvogel's editions were unauthorized ones made from manuscript copies of the composer's works. It is further claimed that de Santis discovered these editions and that he died while actually en route to Amsterdam to confront the publisher.[46]

Until recent times a later French edition of the flute sonatas survived in the Badische Landesbibliothek (formerly the Grossherzogliche Bibliothek) at Karlsruhe. The edition was catalogued by Robert Eitner as follows:

> *XII Sonate a Fl. trav., o V. solo è Bc., o Violoncello . . .*
> Paris [C. N.], LeClerc. Boivin. [Karlsruhe Nr. 57] [47]

Unfortunately, this copy, like other music in the Badische Landesbibliothek was destroyed during World War II. Although the date of the edition is unknown, it is certain that LeClerc issued the work between 1736 and 1740, for it is listed in his catalog which appears in the December, 1740 issue of the *Mercure de France*. Here the collection is briefly identified as the composer's *quatriéme oeuvre* and is priced at eight *livres.*[48]

**SARRI, DOMENICO**

> *Sonata da camera [in fa magg.] à flauto solo, e basso.* Sonata s[econd]da
> I PAc. *Sinfonie* Mss. (CF-V-23), fols. 81r.-82v.

> *Sonata 2a [in sol min.]*
> I PAc. *Sinfonie* Mss. (CF-V-23), fols. 83r.-86r.

> *Sonata 5a [in re magg.]*
> I PAc. *Sinfonie* Mss. (CF-V-23), fols. 86v.-90r.

---

[45] Witvogel, *Catalogus* of 1746. The edition of flute sonatas is listed on page 8. The other works are listed on pages 5, 6, and 14. Some of these editions, including the flute sonatas, were apparently sold by Lotter in Augsburg. See Lotter's *Catalogus* of 1753, pp. 17, 38, and 42.

[46] See François -Joseph Fétis, *Biographie universelle des musiciens,* VII (2nd ed.; Paris: Librairie de Firmin-Didot et Cie, 1875), 395-96 and Eitner, VIII, 421-22.

[47] Eitner, VIII, 422.

[48] Charles Nicholas LeClerc, "Catalogue de musique françoise & italienne," *Mercure de France,* December, 1740, p. 2918. Charles' business began in 1736.

**SOMIS, GIOVANNI BATTISTA**

*Sinfonia [in fa magg.] a flauto solo, e basso*
I PAc. *Sinfonie* Mss. (CF-V-23), fols. 31r.-34r.

**TESSARINI, CARLO**
**Op. II**

Tessarini was a prolific composer whose works are worthy of more attention. Especially needed is a catalog establishing the authenticity and chronology of his works.[49] Presently attributed to him, but not authenticated, is a collection of twelve solo flute sonatas which were apparently first published by Le Cène in 1729. The collection was advertised in the publisher's catalog of 1737 as follows:

547 *XII. Sonate per Flauto traversiere. b. C. da C. Tessarini,*
*opera seconda.*　　　　　　　　　　　　f[lorins] 3.10[50]

The sonatas of this collection are presently known only through later editions and manuscripts (see below).

　　The collection, which is listed in Jean LeClerc's catalog of 1737,[51] should not be confused with *Sei sonate per violino o flauto traversiere e cembalo da Carlo Tessarini,* Op. XIV, an authenticated work that was published by Boivin and J. LeClerc, ca. 1749.

**A Later Edition**

XII SOLOS / *for a* / GERMAN FLUTE / *a* HOBOY *or* VIOLIN / *with a*
*Thorough Bass for the* / HARPSICORD / *or* / BASS VIOLIN / *Compos'd*
*by* / CARLO TESSARINI / DI RIMINI / OPERA SECONDA / / *Note, where*
*these are sold may be had, 12 Concertos for Violins in 6 Parts by the*
*same* / *Author, also great variety of Musick for the German Flute.* / /

---

[49] See the list of works in Albert Dunning, "Tessarini, Carlo," *Die Musik in Geschichte und Gegenwart,* XIII (1966), 261-63.
[50] Le Cène, *Catalogue* of 1737, p. 35.
[51] J. LeClerc, *Catalogue* of 1737, p. 78.

*London. Printed for and Sold by I. Walsh Musick Printer &*
*Instrument maker / to his Majesty at the Harp & Hoboy in*
*Catherine Street in the Strand /* № 580 [1736]

*Source:* **GB** Lbm (g. 688)   Title page and 52 pages of music

*Other copies:* **GB** Cu (MR 380. b. 70. 2); **US** Wc (M 242 .T)

Like Sammartini's works, this opus, probably in Walsh's edition, was widely advertised by other London publishers.

### TESSARINI, CARLO
### Manuscripts

*[Five Sonatas for the Transverse Flute,* from Op. 2*]*
**D-brd** KA. Mss. 948-52.  Separate Parts.

Including Sonatas II, I, VII, XI, and VI.  20 pages of music with separate title pages.

### VALENTINI, GIUSEPPE

*Sinfonia [in do magg.] à flauto solo*
**I** PAc.  *Sinfonie* Mss. (Cf-V-23), fols. 35r.-38r.

*Sonata Ottava [in fa magg.] Sonata da camera à flauto solo, e basso*
**I** PAc.  *Sinfonie* Mss. (CF-V-23), fols. 73r.-74v.

*Sonata 2a [in fa magg.]*
**I** PAc.  *Sinfonie* Mss. (CF-V-23), fols. 75r.-77r.

*Sonata 3a [in fa magg.]*
**I** PAc.  *Sinfonie* Mss. (CF-V-23), fols. 77v.-80r.

### VINCI, LEONARDO

*Twelve* / SOLOS / *For a* / GERMAN FLUTE or VIOLIN / *with a*
*Thorough Bass for the* / HARPSICORD or VIOLONCELLO /
*Compos'd by* / Sigr LEONARDI VINCI / *and other* Italian
Authors. / / London. *Printed for* I. Walsh, *in Catharine Street*
*in the Strand.* / [advertisement follows] . . . [1746]

*Source:* **GB** Lbm (g. 280. b. (17.)) Title page and 31 pages of music

*Other copies:* **A** Wn; **F** Pn (Vm$^7$ 6475); **GB** Ckc, 2 copies (one of them, Rw 16. 61 (1)), Er, Mp, Ob; **S** Skma; **US** NH, Wc, 2 copies (M 241 .V77 and Miller Collection, ML 30.4 1394)

Leonardo Vinci, whose place and date of birth are uncertain, lived all or most of his life in Naples where he died in 1730. Although devoting himself primarily to the writing of operas, for which he became well known, he also wrote a small amount of instrumental music.[52]

In the above collection, Vinci's name appears on the title page only; the sonatas themselves are anonymous. The twelve sonatas are, however, separated into two groups. The first consists of two five-movement sonatas, one in D major and one in G major, printed on pages 1-10. Following a blank, unnumbered page are ten sonatas in three movements that differ from the first ones in style and in their engraving. In short, the collection seems to contain two comparatively early sonatas by Vinci and ten compositions of a new type by "other Italian authors."


## VIVALDI, ANTONIO

*Sonata [in do magg.] a traverso solo*
**GB** Cu. Ms. Add. 7059". 5 pp.

*Sonata [in re min.] a flauto traverso*
**S** Uu. Ms. 7662. 8 pp.

*Sonata [in fa magg.] del Sigr. Vivaldi*
**I** Vqs. Ms. Cl. VIII, Cod. 27, [No. 2]. 4 pp.


## ZANI, ANDREA

*Sonata à flautta è basso*
**D-brd** KA. Ms. 1007.

Of questionable origin, the work consists of the following movements:

$$\text{Cantabile} - \frac{4}{4} - \text{in C major}$$

$$\text{Allegro} - \frac{3}{4} - \text{in C major}$$

$$\text{Minuet and Trio} - \frac{3}{4} - \text{in D major/minor}$$

---

[52] See the biographical sketch and list of works in Helmut Hucke, "Vinci, Leonardo," *Die Musik in Geschichte und Gegenwart,* XIII (1966), 1660-64.

# A LIST OF MODERN EDITIONS

In recent years publishers have issued many new editions of baroque music for the flute and the recorder. Because publication has increased so rapidly, the performer may be acquainted with no more than a fraction of these works. Moreover, it may be difficult for him to determine whether a new publication represents an addition to the repertory or how the edition compares with that of other publications.

The following list will enable readers to survey the Italian solos that have been published since 1900. Perhaps also, if they will examine the list and compare it with the repertory of works presented in the preceding section, they will be encouraged to edit other deserving works.

In order to identify the editions fully and to prevent confusion about the multiple editions of certain works, exact publishers' titles, following the original capitalization except in the use of all capital letters, and edition numbers have been given whenever possible. In addition, the keys have been added in brackets when they do not otherwise appear. Since it has been regrettably impossible to provide annotations, it is hoped that these and other details will enable one to surmise something of the quality of each edition. In this regard the reader may be a part, and, in some cases, the publisher and the date (the date of copyright in most cases). In addition, he should take special notice of the instrumentation. Just as the woodwind player is cautious about an edition that has been prepared for another instrument, especially one prepared for a string instrument, he should be wary of an edition that is arranged for, for example, recorder and piano. For that matter, of course, any edition that is arranged for piano rather than for harpsichord or any of the other traditional *continuo* instruments warrants examination. In most cases the more recent publications, such as those that appear in the series, *Hortus Musicus* (Kassel: Bärenreiter, 1936–) and *Original Music for the Recorder* (Mainz and London: Schott), display more authentic instrumentation, more carefully realized figured basses, and more judicious editing.

The editions are listed alphabetically by composer and, when applicable, according to the order of the works in each first edition of an opus or collection. When several editions of a work exist, they are listed in chronological order. Exceptionally, when a modern edition of a complete opus is available, this edition is listed first.

Naturally, some publications have been prepared from sources other than original first editions. Since information about sources usually may be found in the prefaces to the better editions, remarks about such matters have generally been omitted. For general information about the original sources one should, of course, refer to the list of editions and manuscripts in the preceding section.

## BARSANTI, FRANCESCO

*Sonate a flauto, o violino solo,* [*Op. I, 1724*]

### No. 1

Sonata No. 1 in D Minor for Treble Recorder and Piano (Harpsichord), Violoncello ad lib. Score and parts edited by Walther Bergmann. In the series, *Original Music for the Recorder.* Ed. No. 10555. London: Schott, 1956.

### No. 2

Sonata C-dur für Altblockflöte oder Querflöte und Basso continuo. Score and parts edited by Hugo Ruf. In the series, *Hortus Musicus,* No. 183. Kassel: Bärenreiter, 1964.

### No. 3

Sonata in G Minor for Treble (Alto) Recorder and Piano or Harpsichord with Violoncello ad lib. Score and parts edited by Walther Bergmann. In the series, *Original Music for the Recorder.* Ed. No. 10276. London: Schott, 1954.

### No. 4

Sonate C-moll für Altblockflöte oder Querflöte und Basso continuo. Score and parts edited by Hugo Ruf. In the series, *Hortus Musicus,* No. 184. Kassel: Bärenreiter, 1965.

### No. 5

Sonata in F Major for Treble Recorder and Piano or Harpsichord with Violoncello or Viola da gamba ad lib. Score and parts edited by Walther Bergmann. In the series, *Original Music for the Recorder.* Ed. No. 10075. London: Schott, 1949.

### No. 6

Sonate B-dur für Altblockflöte oder Querflöte und Basso continuo. Score and parts edited by Hugo Ruf. In the series, *Hortus Musicus,* No. 185. Kassel: Bärenreiter, 1965.


## BELLINZANI, PAOLO BENEDETTO

*[XII] Sonate a flauto solo, Op. III, 1720*

### No. 4

Sonate No. IV en sol mineur. Edited by Pierre Poulteau. Paris: Leduc, 1972.

## BONI, GIOVANNI

*Solos for a German Flute* [*ca. 1728*]

Sonata in G [Major] for Oboe and Piano. Containing the first and the fourth movements of No. 1 and the first and the second movements of No. 3. Edited and arranged by Evelyn Rothwell. Ed. No. 441. London: J. & W. Chester, 1968.

## LOCATELLI, PIETRO

*XII Sonate à flauto traversiere solo, Op. II* [*1732*]

### No. 1

Sonata [in C Major]. Edited for flute and piano by J. H. Feltkamp. London: Oxford University Press, 1928.

### No. 2

Sonata II [in D Major] for Flute and Bass. Amsterdam: Broekmans & van Poppel, n.d.

### No. 3

Sonata, E-Dur, für Querflöte und Basso continuo: Cembalo (Pianoforte), Violoncello (Viola da gamba) ad lib. Edited by Hugo Ruf. Ed. No. 5572. Mainz: Schott, 1967.

### No. 4

Sonate I [G-dur]. In *Drei Sonaten für Querflöte und Basso continuo.* Score and parts edited by Gustav Scheck with a realization of the figured bass by Walter Upmeyer. In the series, *Hortus Musicus,* No. 35. Kassel: Bärenreiter, 1949.

Sonata I [G Major]. In *Three Sonatas for Flute and Piano.* Ed. No. 3617. A reprint of the preceding edition. Melville, New York: Belwin Mills, n.d.

Sonata [G-dur] für Flöte (Violine, Oboe) und Gitarre. Edited by Robert Brojer. Vienna: Verlag Doblinger, 1964.

### No. 5

Sonata II [D-dur]. In *Drei Sonaten für Querflöte und Basso continuo.* Score and parts edited by Gustav Scheck with a realization of the figured bass by Walter Upmeyer. In the series, *Hortus Musicus,* No. 35. Kassel: Bärenreiter, 1949.

Sonata II [D Major]. In *Three Sonatas for Flute and Piano.*
Ed. No. 3617. A reprint of the preceding edition. Melville,
New York: Belwin Mills, n.d.

Sonata D-dur für Flöte (Violine, Oboe) und Gitarre. Edited by
Robert Brojer. Vienna: Verlag Doblinger, 1960.

### No. 6

Sonata da camera, G-moll, für Violine und bezifferte Bass.
Edited by Ferdinand David with the basso continuo newly edited
by J. Bachmair. In the series, *Die höhe Schule des Violinspiels.*
Ed. No. 3358. Leipzig: Breitkopf & Härtel, 1957.

Sonata III [G-moll]. In *Drei Sonaten für Querflöte und Basso
continuo.* Score and parts edited by Gustav Scheck with a
realization of the figured bass by Walter Upmeyer. In the series,
*Hortus Musicus,* No. 35. Ed. No. 626. Kassel: Bärenreiter, 1949.

Sonata III [G Minor]. In *Three Sonatas for Flute and Piano.*
Ed. No. 3617. A reprint of the preceding edition. Melville,
New York: Belwin Mills, n.d.

### No. 8

Sonata [in Fa Magg.] per il Flauto Traverso. Edited for flute and piano
by Alexander Kowatscheff. Ed. No. 9000. Zurich: Hug & Co., 1947.

Vester lists three other editions of sonatas, all of them by Deutscher Ricordi.
They contain sonatas in B$^b$ major (No. 3?), C major (no. 1?), and A major (no. 7?).
(See Vester, p. 146.)

**MARCELLO, BENEDETTO**

*Suonate a flauto solo, Op. II, 1712*

A complete edition of the opus, in two volumes, has been published.

*Suonate a Flauto Solo con il suo Basso Continuo per Violoncello
o Cembalo. Opera Seconda. Vol. I: Sonate N 1 a 6. Vol. II:
Sonate N 7 a 12.* Realization of the figured bass by Riccardo Tora.
Revised and edited by Arrigo Tassinari. In the series published
under the direction of Bonaventura Somma, *Musiche Vocali e
Strumentali Sacre e Profane* ec XVII-XVIII-XIX, Nos. 29a-b.
Eds. Nos. 1031 and 1032. Rome: Edizione De Santis, 1964-1966.

## No. 1

Sonata [in F Major] for Flute and Bass. Edited for flute and piano by Joseph Slater. London: Oxford University Press, 1926.

Sonata [in F Major]. In *Two Sonatas for Recorder or Flute (or Oboe) and Keyboard.* Edited by Reba Paeff Mirsky. New York: Hargail Music Press, 1952.

Sonata in Fa Maggiore. In *Quattro Sonate per Flauto (o Oboe) con Accompagnato di Pianoforte.* Revised after the 1948 edition of Giuseppe Martucci by Alberto Veggetti. Ed. No. 722. Rome: Edizioni De Santis, 1955.

Sonata F-dur. In *Zwei Sonaten für Altblockflöte (Querflöte, Violine) und Basso continuo.* Score and parts edited by Jörgen Glode. In the series, *Hortus Musicus,* No. 151. Kassel: Bärenreiter, 1958.

## No. 2

Sonata [in B Minor] Opus I, No. 4. [Opus II, No. 2 transposed for the transverse flute and numbered after the edition of John Walsh published in 1732]. Edited by Jaap Wisse with a realization of the figured bass by Hans Brandt Buys. Published together with Hendrick Focking, Sonata for Flute and Continuo, Opus I, No. 6. Amsterdam: Broekmans & van Poppel, 1949.

Sonata d-moll. In *Zwei Sonaten für Altblockflöte (Querflöte, Violine) und Basso continuo.* Score and parts edited by Jörgen Glode. In the series, *Hortus Musicus,* No. 151. Kassel: Bärenreiter, 1958.

## No. 3

Sonata g-moll. In *Zwei Sonaten für Altblockflöte (Querflöte, Violine) und Basso continuo.* Score and parts edited by Jörgen Glode. In the series, *Hortus Musicus,* No. 142. Kassel: Bärenreiter, 1956.

## No. 4

Sonate e-moll. In *Zwei Sonaten für Altblockflöte, (Querflöte, Violine) und Basso continuo.* Score and parts edited by Jörgen Glode. In the series, *Hortus Musicus,* No. 142. Kassel: Bärenreiter, 1956.

Sonata e-moll Nr. 4. In *3 Sonaten für Blockflöte und Continuo.* Score and parts edited by L. Höffer von Winterfeld and K. H. Stolze. Ed. No. 471. Hamburg: H. Sikorski, 1957.

## No. 5

Sonata XII [in G Major] for flute and piano. Edited by Joseph Slater. London: Oxford University Press, 1950.

Sonata [G-dur] für Flöte und Klavier. Edited by Herman Zanke.
Ed. No. 11830. Frankfurt am Main: Wilhelm Zimmermann, 1954.

Sonata in Sol Maggiore. In *Quattro Sonate per Flauto (o Oboe)*
*con Accompagnato di Pianoforte.* Revised after the 1948 edition
of Giuseppe Martucci by Alberto Veggetti. Ed. No. 722. Rome:
Edizioni De Santis, 1955.

Sonata G-dur für Querflöte (Violine) Cembalo (B. c.) und Cello ad
libitum. Score and parts edited by Rolf Ermeler with a realization
of the figured bass by Manfred Kluge. Ed. No. 3279. Wilhelmshaven:
O. H. Noetzel, 1962.

### No. 6

Sonata C-dur Nr. 6. In *3 Sonaten für Blockflöte und Continuo.*
Score and parts edited by L. Höffer von Winterfeld and K. H. Stolze.
Ed. No. 471. Hamburg: H. Sikorski, 1957.

Sonata C-dur. In *Zwei Sonaten für Altblockflöte (Querflöte, Violine)*
*und Basso continuo.* Score and parts edited by Jörgen Glode. In the
series, *Hortus Musicus,* No. 152. Kassel: Bärenreiter, 1958.

### No. 7

Sonata in B Flat [Major] for Flute (or Treble Recorder) or Violin.
Edited for flute and piano by William Pearson. London: Oxford
University Press, 1957.

Sonata B-dur. In *Zwei Sonaten für Altblockflöte (Querflöte, Violine)*
*und Basso continuo.* Score and parts edited by Jörgen Glode. In the
series, *Hortus Musicus,* No. 152. Kassel: Bärenreiter, 1958.

Sonata B-Dur für Querflöte (Violine) Cembalo (B. c.) und Cello ad
libitum. Score and parts edited by Rolf Ermeler with a realization
of the figured bass by Manfred Kluge. Ed. No. 3277. Wilhelmshaven:
O. H. Noetzel, 1962.

### No. 8

Sonata in Re Minore. In *Quattro Sonate per Flauto (o Oboe) con*
*Accompagnato di Pianoforte.* Revised after the 1948 edition of
Giuseppe Martucci by Alberto Veggetti. Ed. No. 722. Rome: Edizioni
De Santis, 1955.

Sonate d-Moll für Altblockflöte (Querflöte, Violine) und Basso continuo.
Score and parts edited by Hugo Ruf. In the series, *Originalmusik für die*
*Blockflöte.* Ed. No. 5341. Mainz: Schott, 1965.

No. 9

Sonata C-dur Nr. 9. In *3 Sonaten für Blockflöte und Continuo.*
Score and parts edited by L. Höffer von Winterfeld and K. H.
Stolze. Ed. No. 471. Hamburg: H. Sikorski, 1957.

No. 10

Sonata a-moll für Querflöte (Violine) Cembalo (B. c.) and Cello ad
libitum. Score and parts edited by Rolf Ermeler with a realization of
the figured bass by Manfred Kluge. Ed. No. 3278. Wilhelmshaven:
O. H. Noetzel, 1962.

Sonate a-Moll für Altblockflöte (Querflöte, Violine) und Basso
continuo. Score and parts edited by Hugo Ruf. In the series,
*Originalmusik für die Blockflöte.* Ed. No. 5342. Mainz: Schott, 1965.

No. 11

Sonata [in G Minor]. In *Two Sonatas for Recorder or Flute (or Oboe)
and Keyboard.* Edited by Reba Paeff Mirsky. New York: Hargail
Music Press, 1952.

Sonata in Sol Minore. In *Quattro Sonate per Flauto (o Oboe) con
Accompagnato di Pianoforte.* Revised after the 1948 edition of
Giuseppe Martucci by Alberto Veggetti. Ed. No. 722. Rome: Edizioni
De Santis, 1955.

PLATTI, GIOVANNI

*Sei Sonate a flauto traversiere solo, Op. III [1743?]*

No. 1

Sonate D-dur für Flauto traverso und Basso continuo. Score and parts
edited by Gustav Scheck and Hugo Ruf. In the series, *Florilegium
musicum,* No. 9. Ed. No. Sy 520. Lörrach: Deutscher Ricordi, 1955.

No. 2

Sonate G dur für Flöte und Klavier. Edited by Phillip Jarnach. In the
series, *Antiqua, eine Sammlung alter Musik.* Ed. No. 377. Mainz:
Schott, 1924.

Adagio and Allegro; 3rd and 4th movements from Sonata II in G Major
for flute and piano. Edited and arranged by George Waln. Ed. No.
S-700-4-1. Chicago: Neil A. Kjos Music Co., 1945.

## No. 3

Sonate e moll für Flöte und Klavier. Edited by Phillip Jarnach. In the series, *Antiqua, eine Sammlung alter Musik.* Ed. No. 376. Mainz: Schott, 1924.

## No. 4

Sonata A dur für Flöte und Klavier. Edited by Philipp Jarnach. In the series, *Antiqua, eine Sammlung alter Musik.* Ed. No. 2457. Mainz: Schott, 1936.

Sonate A-Dur für Flauto traverso und Basso continuo. Score and parts edited by Hugo Ruf. In the series, *Florilegium musicum.* Ed. No. Sy 582. Lörrach: Deutscher Ricordi, 1954.

## No. 6

Sonate G-dur für Flöte und Basso continuo. Score and parts edited by Hugo Ruf. Ed. No. 4183. Mainz: Schott, 1963.

Vester lists two other editions of sonatas, one of a sonata in G major (either no. 2 or no. 5) and one of a sonata in C minor (*sic*; probably no. 5 in C major). Both are published by Deutscher Ricordi. (See Vester, p. 184.)

**SAMMARTINI, GIUSEPPE**

*Sonate a solo et a due flauti traversi, Op. I* [*1736*]

## No. 1

Sonate in E moll für Violine mit beziffertem Bass. In the series edited by Alfred Moffat, *Meisterschule der alten Zeit,* No. 41. Ed. No. 1068. Berlin: Simrock, 1929.

Sonata (Nr. 1 E-moll) für Flöte (Blockflöte). Edited by F. J. Giesbert. Neuwied am Rhein: Pfauen-Verlag, 1951.

## No. 2

Sonata (Nr. 2 G-dur) für Flöte (Blockflöte). Edited by F. J. Giesbert. Neuwied am Rhein: Pfauen-Verlag, 1951.

## No. 4

Sonata . . . A moll . . . In the series edited by Alfred Moffat, *Kammer-Sonaten für Violine und Pianoforte des 17ten und 18ten Jahrhunderts,* No. 16. Mainz: Schott, 1910.

*XII Sonate a flauto traversiere solo, Opus II* [*1736?*]

### No. 4

Sonata in G [Major] for Oboe and Piano. Edited by Evelyn Rothwell
with a realization of the figured bass by A. Gibilaro. Ed. No. 1575.
London: J. & W. Chester, 1951.

## TESSARINI, CARLO

*XII Sonate per flauto traversiere, Op. II* [*1729*]

### No. 7

Sonate F-dur für Flöte und Basso continuo. Edited by Hans-Peter
Schmitz and M. Schneider. Ed. No. 3303. Kassel: Bärenreiter, 1956.

Vester lists two other editions of sonatas by Tessarini, one in C major published
by Ernst Vogel and one in D major by Wilhelm Zimmermann. Although both
publications apparently are edited for flute, it is uncertain whether they are
from Opus II. (See Vester, p. 235.)

## VINCI, LEONARDO

*Twelve Solos for a German Flute or Violin* [*1746*]

### No. 1

Sonata in D Major. London: Oxford University Press, 1926.

Sonate [en re majeur]. In the collection, *Oeuvres originales des
xvii$^e$ et xviii$^e$ siècles pour la flûte.* Edited for flute and piano by
L. Fleury. Ed. No. 17361. Paris: Leduc, 1928.

Sonate für Flöte und Continuo (Cembalo) in D-dur. Edited by
Joseph Bopp. Basel: Ernst Reinhardt Verlag AG [1949?]

### No. 2

Sonata für Flöte und Continuo (Cembalo) in G-dur. Edited by
Joseph Bopp. Basel: Ernst Reinhardt Verlag AG [1955].

Sonata in G Major for Flute and Piano. Ed. No. 4078. A reprint
of the preceding edition? Melville, New York: Belwin Mills, n.d.

**VIVALDI, ANTONIO**

*Sonata [in do magg.] a traversa solo*
Cambridge. University Library. Ms. Add. 7059''.

Sonata [in Do Magg.] Per Flauto Traverso e Continuo. Edited for flute and piano or harpsichord by Millicent Silver. Ed. No. 1577. London: J. & W. Chester, 1952.

Sonata, C-dur, für Querflöte (Violine) und Basso continuo. Edited by Frank Nagel with a realization of the figured bass by Winfried Radeke. In the series, *L'Arte del Flauto*. Wilhelmshaven: Heinrichshofen, 1970.

The work appears to be published by Wilhelm Hansen also. (See Vester, p. 245.)

*Sonata [in re min.] a flauto traverso*
Uppsala. Universitetsbibliotek. Ms. 7662.

Sonata, d-moll, für Querflöte (Violine) und Basso continuo. Edited by Frank Nagel with a realization of the figured bass by Winfried Radeke. In the series, *L'Arte del Flauto*. Wilhelmshaven: Heinrichshofen, 1970.

*Sonata [in fa magg.] del Sig. Vivaldi.*
Venice. Biblioteca dell' Accademia Querini-Stampalia. Ms. Cl. VIII. Cod. 27, [No. 2].

Sonata [in F Major] for Flute and Piano. Edited by John Edmunds. Ed. No. 3010-12. Boston: R. D. Row Music Co., 1956.

Sonata [in F Major]. Edited by Frans Brüggen. Ed. No. 517. Amsterdam: Broekmans & van Poppel, 1959.

Sonata F-dur. In *Zwei Sonaten für Blockflöte (oder Querflote, Oboe, Violine) und Beziffertem Bass (Klavier, Cembalo mit Violoncello oder Gambe ad lib.)*. Score and parts edited by Walter Kolneder. Ed. No. 2119. Heidelberg: Willy Müller, Süddeutscher Musikverlag, 1962.

Sonata F-Dur für Altblockflöte und Basso Continuo. Edited by Frank Nagel with a realization of the figured bass by Winfried Radeke. In the series, *Originalmusik für die Blöckflote*. Mainz: Schott, 1971.

# Appendix
# THREE COMPOSERS
# WHOSE FLUTE SONATAS
# ARE BELIEVED LOST

## BALDINI, [GIROLAMO?]

The composer has not been firmly identified. Fétis speaks of a Jérôme Baldini who was born in Verona and who came to Paris during the first half of the seventeenth century where he taught flute. He adds that the man was also known for a book of solo flute sonatas.[1] Robert Eitner and Carlo Schmidl provide the same information; however, they use the Italian forename, Girolamo.[2] Eitner also questions the statement that Baldini came to Paris in the first half of the seventeenth century, implying that this period is approximately one hundred years too early for the solo flute sonata, certainly in France.

Eitner is no doubt correct that Baldini's period of activity has been erroneously dated. One may assume that the person to whom Fétis refers is identical with the one whose last name appears in the catalogs of J. LeClerc, and Boivin and Ballard, dating from 1742. Both catalogs list a single book of solo sonatas for the flute price at four *livres*.[3] Like the flutist identified by Fétis, this man seems to have no other compositions ascribed to him.

---

[1] Fétis, I, 228.
[2] Eitner, I, 314 and Schmidl, I, 101.
[3] J. LeClerc, *Catalogue* of 1742, p. 56 and Christophe-Jean-François Ballard and Mme. Boivin, *Catalogue général et alphabétique de musique, imprimée ou gravée en France* (Paris: 1742; Bib. Nat., Q 9038), p. 3.

## TORTORITI, GABRIELE

Gabriele Tortoriti lived sometime during the first half of the eighteenth century, judging from publishers' catalogs and editions of music that bear his name. It appears that he may have worked for a time in England, for all, or at least most of his known works—a collection of twelve sonatas for the flute, a collection of duets for violin and flute, and a collection of trio sonatas—were published in London by John Simpson. Although certain works were issued by other publishers, the collection of flute sonatas is listed exclusively in Simpson's catalogs, one of which dates ca. 1745 and contains the following entry.

> *Twelve Solos for a German Flute and a Bass. Composed by Sigr. Tortoriti . . .* 3 [shillings] -0 [pence].[4]

## URSILLO, FABIO

Fabio Ursillo, often identified in eighteenth-century sources merely by his first name, was born in Rome during the end of the seventeenth century. In 1725 he entered the service of the Bishop of Tournai, whom he served until his death in 1759. Travelling to Brussels and other centers in the Low Countries, he became known as a virtuoso of the archlute, guitar, violin, and the flute. Although Fabio's trio sonatas are perhaps his best known works now,[5] he is also the author of two collections of flute sonatas. The first collection, identified as his *premier livre,* was published probably ca. 1731, judging from an early privilege.[6] The other collection, identified as his *quatriéme livre,* was listed apparently for the first time in 1742 in the catalogs of J. LeClerc, and Boivin and Ballard.[7]

---

[4] See John Simpson, "A Catalogue of New Musick," appended to *The Delightful Pocket Companion* (London [ca. 1745]; Brit. Mus., d. 56.), p. 3. All three collections are listed here and also in John Cox, "A Catalogue of New Musick" (London: John Cox at Simpson's Musick Shop [ca. 1755]; Brit. Mus., Hirsch IV. 1113. (3.)), [p. 1].

[5] For a biographical sketch, a list of extant works, and a bibliography, see Francesco Degrada, "Ursillo, Fabio," *Die Musik in Geschichte und Gegenwart,* XIII (1966), 1178-79.

[6] See Michel Brenet, "La Librairie musicale en France de 1653 à 1790, d'après les registres de privilèges," *Sammelbände der Internationalen Musikgesellschaft,* VIII (1906-1907), 433 and J. LeClerc, *Catalogue* of 1737, p. 56.

[7] J. LeClerc, *Catalogue* of 1737, p. 56 and *Catalogue* of 1742, p. 54, and Boivin and Ballard, *Catalogue* of 1742, p. 27. An edition of flute sonatas apparently was published in Amsterdam, also. See Vester, p. 241.

# BIBLIOGRAPHY

ALKER, Hugo. *Blockflöten-Bibliographie.* Wilhelmshaven: Heinrichshofen, 1966.

——. *Blockflöten-Bibliographie, 2; Nachtrag und Gesamtregister.* Wilhelmshaven: Heinrichshofen, 1969.

BALLARD, Christophe-Jean-François, and Mme. Boivin. *Catalogue général et alphabétique de musique, imprimée ou gravée en France.* Paris: 1742. Bib. Nat., Q 9038.

BLUME, Friedrich, ed. *Die Musik in Geschichte und Gegenwart: Allgemeine Enzyklopädie der Musik.* (15 vols. to date) Kassel, Basel: Bärenreiter-Verlag, 1949-

BREITKOPF und HÄRTEL. *The Breitkopf Thematic Catalogue, 1762-1787.* Facsimile edition. Edited by Barry S. Brook. New York: Dover, 1966.

BREMNER, Robert. "A Catalogue of Vocal and Instrumental Music." London: March, 1782. Brit. Mus., Hirsch IV. 1112. (2.).

BRENET, Michel. "La Libraire musicale en France de 1653 à 1790, d'après les registres de privilèges." *Sammelbände der Internationalen Musikgesellschaft,* VIII (1906-1907), 401-66.

*The British Union Catalogue of Early Music Printed Before the Year 1801.*
2 vols. London: Butterworths Scientific Publications, 1957.

BURNEY, Charles. *A General History of Music.* 4 vols. London: By the Author,
1776-1789.

CAVALLI, Alberto. "Canuti, Giovanni Antonio." *Die Musik in Geschichte und
Gegenwart,* XV (1973), 1297.

CLERCX, Suzanne. "Fiocco." *Die Musik in Geschichte und Gegenwart,* IV
(1955), 248-53.

CONCINA, Giovanni (comp.). *Catalogo della Biblioteca Querini-Stampalia di
Venezia.* Vol. VI of *Catalogo general . . .* Published by the Associazione
dei Musicologi Italiani. Parma: Freschig, 1914.

COX, John. "A Catalogue of New Musick." London: John Cox at Simpson's
Musick Shop [ca. 1755]. Brit. Mus., Hirsch IV. 1113. (3.).

————. "A Catalogue of Vocal and Instrumental Music." Appended to Felice
Giardini. *Sei Sonate di cembalo con violino o flauto traverso.* Opera
Terza. London [ca. 1751]. Brit. Mus., Hirsch III. 225.

CUCUËL, Georges. "Quelques documents sur la librairie musicale au XVIIIe
siècle." *Sammelbände der Internationalen Musikgesellschaft,* XIII (1911-
1912), 385-92.

DEGRADA, Francesco. "Ursillo, Fabio." *Die Musik in Geschichte und
Gegenwart,* XIII (1966), 1178-79.

DUNNING, Albert. *De muziekuitgever Gerhard Fredrik Witvogel en zijn fonds.*
Vol. II of *Muziekhistorische Monografieën.* Published by the Vereniging
voor Nederlandse Muziekgeschiedenis. Utrecht: A. Oosthoek, 1966.

————. "Tessarini, Carlo." *Die Musik in Geschichte und Gegenwart,* XIII (1966),
260-64.

DUNNING, Albert, and KOOLE, Arend. "Pietro Antonio Locatelli; Nieuwe
bijdragen tot de kennis van zijn leven en werken." *Tijdschrift van de
Vereniging voor Nederlandse Muziekgeschiedenis,* XX/nos. 1-2 (1964-
1965), 52-96.

ÉCORCHEVILLE, Jules. *Catalogue du fonds de musique ancienne de la
Bibliothèque Nationale.* 8 vols. Paris: J. Terquem & Cie, 1910-1914.

EITNER, Robert. *Biographisch-Bibliographisches Quellen-Lexikon der Musiker und Musikgelehrten.* 10 vols. Leipzig: Breitkopf & Härtel, 1900-1904.

FÉTIS, François-Joseph. *Biographie universelle des musiciens.* 8 vols. 2nd ed. Paris: Librairie de Firmin-Didot et Cie, 1873-1875.

GASPARI, Gaetano (comp.). *Catalogo della Biblioteca del Liceo Musicale di Bologna.* 5 vols. Bologna: Libreria Romagnoli dall'Acqua and Regia Tipografia Fratelli Merlani, 1890-1943.

GASPERINI, Guido, and PELLICELLI, Nestore (comps.). *Catalogo delle città di Parma e Reggio.* Vol. I of *Catalogo generale . . .* Published by the Associazione dei Musicologi Italiani. Parma: Freschig, 1911.

GERBER, Ernst Ludwig. *Historisch-biographisches Lexicon der Tonkünstler.* 2 vols. Leipzig: J. G. I. Breitkopf, 1790-1792.

———. *Neues historisch-biographisches Lexikon der Tonkünstler.* 4 vols. Leipzig: A. Kuehnel, 1812-1814.

GERICKE, Hannelore. *Der Wiener Musikalienhandel von 1700 bis 1778.* Vol. V of *Wiener musikwissenschaftliche Beiträge.* Graz: H. Böhlaus Nachf., 1960.

HOFFMANN-ERBRECHT, Lothar. "Der Nürnburger Musikverlager Johann Ulrich Haffner." *Acta musicologica,* XXVI (1954), 114-26.

———. "Platti, Giovanni Benedetto." *Die Musik in Geschichte und Gegenwart,* X (1962), 1341-42.

HUCKE, Helmut. "Vinci, Leonardo." *Die Musik in Geschichte und Gegenwart,* XIII (1966), 1660-64.

JOHNSON, John. "A Catalogue of Vocal and Instrumental Music, 1770, Printed and Sold by John Johnson, at the Harp and Crown in Cheapside, London." Brit. Mus., Hirsch IV. 1111. (10.).

———. "A Catalogue of Vocal and Instrumental Musick." London [ca. 1754]. Brit. Mus., Hirsch IV. 1111. (9.).

KIDSON, Frank. *British Music Publishers, Printers and Engravers.* London: W. E. Hill & Sons, 1900.

KÖCHEL, Ludwig von. *Die kaiserliche Hof-Musikkapelle zu Wien von 1543 bis 1867.* Vienna: Beck'sche Universitätsbuchhandlung, 1869.

KOOLE, Arend J. *Pietro Locatelli da Bergamo.* Amsterdam: Jasonpers, 1949.

LaBORDE, Jean Benjamine de. *Essai sur la musique ancienne et moderne.* 4 vols. Paris: Eugene Onfroy, 1780.

Le CÈNE, Michel-Charles. *Catalogue des livres de musique imprimés à Amsterdam, chez Michel Charles Le Cène.* Amsterdam [1737]. Gemeentemuseum, Scheurleer Collection, 4 B 59.

LeCLERC, Charles Nicholas. "Catalogue de musique françoise & italienne." *Mercure de France,* December, 1740, pp. 2917-20.

LeCLERC, Jean. *Catalogue de musique tant françoise qu' italiene imprimée ou gravée en France à Paris chez le Sieur Le Clerc.* Paris: 1742. Bib. Nat. Q 9037.

————. *Catalogue général de musique imprimée ou gravée en France ensemble de celle qui est gravée ou imprimée dans les pays étrangers . . . se vend à Paris chez le Sieur le Clerc.* Paris: 1737. Bib. Nat., Q 9036.

LESURE, François. *Bibliographie des éditions musicales publiées par Estienne Roger et Michel-Charles Le Cène (Amsterdam, 1696-1743).* Vol. XII of *Publications de la Société Française de Musicologie,* Series II. Paris: Société Française de Musicologie, 1969.

LOONAN, Martin A. "A Listing of Late Baroque Solo Sonatas for Alto Recorder." *The American Recorder,* XII/no. 3 (August 1971), 86-90.

LOTTER, Jacob, the Younger. *Catalogus aller musikalischen Bücher* (1753). Facsimile edition. Edited by Adolph Layer. Vol. II of *Catalogus Musicus.* Kassel: Bärenreiter, 1964.

————. *Musikalischer Catalogus aller derjenigen Bücher und Musicalien.* Augsburg: 1773. Brit. Mus., Hirsch IV. 1108. a.

McGOWAN, Richard A. "Italian Baroque Solo Sonatas for the Recorder and the Flute." Unpublished Ph.D. dissertation, University of Michigan, 1974.

MARTINOTTI, Sergio. "Brivio, Giuseppe Ferdinando." *Die Musik in Geschichte und Gegenwart,* XV (1973), 1093-94.

MELL, Albert. "Dall' Oglio." *Die Musik in Geschichte und Gegenwart,* IX (1961), 1913-16.

MISHKIN, Henry G. "The Published Instrumental Works of Giovanni Battista Sammartini: A Bibliographical Reappraisal." *The Musical Quarterly,* XLV/no. 3 (July 1959), 361-74.

NETTL, Paul. *Forgotten Musicians.* New York: Philosophical Library, 1951.

PELLICELLI, Nestore. "Musicisti in Parma nel sec. XVIII.—La Cappella della Steccata—La Cappella Corale della Cattedrale." *Note d' archivio per la storia musicale,* XI/no. 1 (January-March 1934), 29-57.

PETROBELLI, Pierluigi. "Bellinzani, Paolo Benedetto." *Die Musik in Geschichte und Gegenwart,* XV (1973), 629-30.

PINCHERLE, Marc. *Corelli, His Life, His Work.* Translated from the French by Hubert E. M. Russell. New York: W. W. Norton & Co., Inc., 1956.

QUANTZ, Johann Joachim. "Herrn Johann Joachim Quantzens Lebenslauf, von ihm selbst entworfen." Published in Friedrich Wilhelm Marpurg. *Historisch-kritische Beyträge zur Aufnahme der Musik,* Vol. IV. Berlin: Johann Jacob Schuetzens sel. Wittwe, 1755.

*Répertoire internationale des sources musicales.* Series A: *Einzeldrucke vor 1800.* (6 vols. to date) Munich: G. Henle, 1971-    .

*Répertoire internationale des sources musicales.* Series B, Vol. II: *Recueils imprimés du xviii$^e$ siècle.* Munich: G. Henle, 1964.

ROGER, Estienne. "Catalogue des livres de musique nouvellement imprimez à Amsterdam chez Estienne Roger Marchand Libraire." Appended to Jean François Félibien. *Recueil historique de la vie et des ouvrages des plus celebres architects.* Amsterdam [1706].

SCHMIDL, Carlo. *Dizionario universale dei musicisti.* 2 vols. and suppl. Milan: Casa Editrice Sonzogno, 1928, 1929, and 1938.

SIMPSON, John. "A Catalogue of New Musick." Appended to *The Delightful Pocket Companion.* London [ca. 1745]. Brit. Mus., d. 56.

SMITH, William C., and HUMPHRIES, Charles. *A Bibliography of the Musical Works Published by the Firm of John Walsh during the Years 1721-1766.* London: The Bibliographical Society, 1968.

———. *Handel: A Descriptive Catalogue of the First Editions.* 2nd ed. New York: Barnes and Noble, 1970.

SPRINGER, H., SCHNEIDER, M., and WOLFFHEIM, W. *Miscellanea Musicae Bio-bibliographica,* Vol. II. New York: Musurgia, 1947.

STELLFELD, Christiane. *Les Fiocco, une famille musiciens belge aux xvii$^e$ et xviii$^e$ siècles.* Vol. VII of *Académie royale de Belgique, Classe des Beaux-Arts, Mémoires,* Series II. Bruxelles: Palais des Académies, 1941.

THOMPSON, Peter. "A Catalogue of Musick." London [ca. 1752]. Brit. Mus., Hirsch IV. 1111. (14.).

TILMOUTH, Michael. *A Calendar of References to Music in Newspapers Published in London and the Provinces. Royal Musical Association Research Chronicle No. 1.* 1961.

VESTER, Frans. *Flute Repertoire Catalogue.* London: Musica Rara, 1967.

WALTHER, Johann Gottfried. *Musicalisches Lexicon.* Facsimile of the original edition of 1732. Edited by Richard Schaal. Vol. III of *Documenta musicologica,* Series I. Kassel: Bärenreiter, 1953.

WINTERFELD, Linde Höffer von. *Handbuch der Blockflöten-Literatur.* Berlin: Bote & Bock, 1959.

WITVOGEL, Gerhard Fredrik. *Catalogus van een uitmuntende verzameling van een groote extra fraaije gedrukte partye exemplaren van nieuw musicq.* Amsterdam: Arent Rampen, 1746. Gemeentemuseum, Scheurleer Collection.

# INDEX OF COMPOSERS